EMPOWERING THE BEGINNING TEACHER OF MATHEMATICS IN
HIGH SCHOOL

EMPOWERING THE BEGINNING TEACHER OF MATHEMATICS

A series edited by Michaele F. Chappell

EMPOWERING THE BEGINNING TEACHER OF MATHEMATICS IN

HIGH SCHOOL

Edited by

Michaele F. Chappell
Middle Tennessee State University
Murfreesboro, Tennessee

Jeffrey Choppin
University of Rochester
Rochester, New York

Jenny Salls
Washoe County School District
Sparks, Nevada

NCTM

NATIONAL COUNCIL OF
TEACHERS OF MATHEMATICS

Library of Congress Cataloging-in-Publication Data

Empowering the beginning teacher of mathematics in high school /
edited by Michaele F. Chappell, Jeffrey Choppin, Jenny Salls.
        p. cm. — (Empowering the beginning teacher of mathematics)
    Includes bibliographical references.
    ISBN 0-87353-561-8
    1. Mathematics—Study and teaching (Secondary) I. Chappell,
Michaele F. II. Choppin, Jeffrey. III. Salls, Jenny. IV. Series.
    QA11.2.E47 2004
    510'.71'2—dc22

                                    2004001873

CONTENTS

INDUCTION AND MENTORING OF NEW TEACHERS

Position

The National Council of Teachers of Mathematics believes that school systems and universities must assume the shared responsibility for the sustained professional support of beginning teachers by providing them with a structured induction and mentoring program. This effort must include opportunities for further development of mathematics content, pedagogy, and management strategies. Association with a trained mentor who has a strong background in mathematics, mathematics pedagogy, and classroom practice is crucial to this program.

Background and Rationale

"Before It's Too Late," a report of the National Commission on Science and Mathematics Teaching in the 21st Century, recommended that teachers be initiated into the profession through induction programs. In many school settings, new mathematics teachers who may not have strong mathematics content knowledge are isolated and given little support and content-specific professional development. In these circumstances, their students are not afforded the learning opportunities and quality instruction advocated by the Council.

The retention of new teachers continues to be a problem, contributing to the overall shortage of mathematics teachers. A research review by Yvonne Gold found that 30 to 37 percent of new teachers leave the profession within their first five years ("Beginning Teacher Support: Attrition, Mentoring, and Induction," in *Handbook of Research on Teacher Education*, 2nd ed., edited by John Sikula, Thomas Buttery, and Edith Guyton [New York: Macmillan, 1996], pp. 548–94).

Recommendations

- School systems should develop structured induction programs that include mentoring.
- University teacher-preparation programs should serve as a partner with school districts in induction programs by participating in the training of mentors, continuing communication with their graduates, and serving as a resource.
- Mentor teachers should be provided with significant and consistent training and be given additional remuneration or release time for their services.
- Schools should set aside time specifically for the collaborative efforts of the beginning teacher and the mentor.
- District and school administrators should recognize the added demands on beginning teachers and their mentors and should be sensitive in making teaching assignments.
- Districts and universities should offer professional development that includes a strong focus on content knowledge, pedagogical knowledge, pedagogical content knowledge, and a knowledge of *Principles and Standards for School Mathematics* and its applications to the classroom.

(August 2002)

PREFACE
Yes, you have made a great career choice as a teacher!

—Shirley M. Frye

Teaching is a rewarding profession. As you embark on what may be the most important adventure of your life—that is, the process of teaching students mathematics—take comfort in the words of Shirley Frye, NCTM Past President, spoken at the Beginning Teachers Conference held at the NCTM Eastern Regional Conference in Boston, Massachusetts, in November 2002. Have confidence in the knowledge that you have acquired from your educational experiences thus far. Exercise patience with yourself as you strive to achieve higher levels of competence and reach proficiency.

As you begin your journey as a teacher of mathematics, you are likely to encounter challenges—both inside and outside the classroom—that will seem to overshadow the perceived rewards of teaching. Realize that in your early years of teaching mathematics, you will probably have a "large learning agenda" (Feiman-Nemser 2003, p. 27) that may require you to gain more knowledge about the content you are teaching and how best to present it to your students. This agenda may also require that you learn more about the norms of teaching among your colleagues and in your school community. Although obstacles will surface during your early years of teaching, you should view them as unique learning opportunities that enable you to refine your existing skills and polish your daily practices as you progress along the path of mastery in your new career.

To assist you in this process, the Editorial/Author Panel for the Needs of Mathematics Teachers Beginning Their Careers has compiled this high school volume to help you reach your full potential as an effective teacher of mathematics, thereby improving the mathematics learning of the students who will be the recipients of your instruction throughout your career. The Empowering the Beginning Teacher of Mathematics series contains three books geared specifically toward elementary, middle, and high school teachers of mathematics. These books have been written both *for* you and *to* you. Several authors present their discussions objectively, with the beginning teacher in mind, but many share their wisdom and insights as if they were conversing with you over a cup of tea. We hope that this level of familiarity will set the tone for your use of this volume.

Our initial charge and primary goal was to develop a resource to which beginning teachers of mathematics could refer and one that they would use often while attending to the many demands of the classroom and the teaching profession in general. We all know that each academic year brings new faces and new demands to the classroom, at times making even veteran teachers feel like beginners again. Thus, we anticipate that this volume may also serve as a source of inspiration for both beginning teachers and their more experienced colleagues.

The Panel has aimed to produce a unique resource that highlights varied contributions in six broad categories: (1) professional growth, (2) curriculum and instruction, (3) classroom-level assessment, (4) classroom management and organization, (5) equity, and (6) school and community. To us, these categories represent the essential domains to which beginning teachers of mathematics must give immediate attention during the early years to establish a firm foundation in the classroom and to pave the way for a long tenure in mathematics teaching. In each category, individual contributions take on different formats, including featured articles, related thematic ideas, bulleted lists of tips and advice, personal testimonies, quick notes that shed light on specific topics, and quotable thoughts that can be stated best only by teachers. Journal-like pages are included at the end of each section for you to make notes and add your personal ideas, stories, tips, or advice to which you can refer in subsequent years or share with colleagues.

From the onset of the writing project, we were careful to avoid producing a volume that mirrors the numerous resources already available in teacher journals and related books. We certainly encourage you, as a beginning teacher of mathematics, to make full use of these resources as you seek to learn more about the situations you encounter in your first few months in the classroom. Our desire, however, is that you do more than merely "read and shelve" this publication. We hope that you keep it close at hand during your early years as a teacher and that you think of it as an *active* resource—one that becomes an integral part of your teaching regimen—in your search for solutions to issues and problems, not solely mathematical, that are sure to arise in your classroom or school during your beginning years.

Numerous people have made possible the production of the books in the Empowering the Beginning Teacher of Mathematics series. I especially offer my gratitude to the other members of the Editorial/Author Panel for their innovative, diligent, and focused work:

- Jeffrey M. Choppin, University of Rochester, Rochester, New York

- Tina Pateracki, Jasper County Schools, Ridgeland, South Carolina

- Jenny Salls, Washoe County School District, Sparks, Nevada

- Jane F. Schielack, Texas A&M University, College Station, Texas

- Sharon Zagorski, Milwaukee Public Schools, Milwaukee, Wisconsin

Throughout this project, the members of the Panel have contributed countless hours reviewing, editing, and crafting supporting segments to prepare this entire volume for *you*—the beginning teacher of mathematics in the high school. I also wish to acknowledge Harry Tunis, our staff liaison at the National Council of Teachers of Mathematics (NCTM), for his unwavering support and guidance, as well as the production staff of NCTM for assistance in the editing and production of this work. Finally, I wish to thank the authors, who have contributed to this effort as a response to their own desire to see you develop into an enthusiastic, effective classroom practitioner.

Our hope in producing this volume is that you "emerge from [your] first few years of teaching [mathematics] feeling empowered, supported, and capable in all roles of the classroom teacher" (Renard 2003, p. 64). You can help yourself in this endeavor by recognizing the multi-faceted roles and responsibilities that teachers of mathematics assume during their beginning years. Moreover, as NCTM's position statement about new teachers suggests, you should, if possible, take part in a high-quality induction or mentoring program. Ultimately, you should position yourself to reach out to your future colleagues who will enter the field after you and share the ideas that you learn from this volume, other resources, and your own experience.

Yes, you have made a great career choice as a teacher of mathematics in the high school. Now we urge you to enjoy your journey!

Michaele F. Chappell
Series Editor

INTRODUCTION

Jeffrey Choppin
Jenny Salls

As a beginning teacher of high school mathematics, you will be expected to draw on all the skills and knowledge you learned in your teacher education and mathematics classes and, more than likely, some abilities and talents that you did not acquire in college. Your teaching assignment may call for you to teach a wide variety of subjects—from remedial to advanced mathematics—to students from increasingly diverse backgrounds in schools with widely differing missions. This book, consisting of ideas and advice from experienced educators, has been written to help you hone your skills and work productively during the beginning years as you focus on the essential aspects of teaching mathematics in a high school environment.

Often, teaching requires a dual focus on global trends and ideas, as well as issues that arise in your specific circumstances. Global trends may include changes in the nature of mathematics reform, shifts in national education policies, or world events that alter your students' perspectives and, possibly, the makeup of your school's population. Such trends can affect the methods you use both to teach mathematics and to assess your students' learning.

Your individual circumstances include the students with whom you interact daily, the curriculum you teach, and the physical space you use as a classroom. For example, we all know that high school students have fairly strong perceptions about mathematics and their own mathematical abilities. Thus, as students progress through high school, they make important decisions about which mathematics courses they will take and how well they will perform in these courses. Whether they are aware of it, the decisions they make in high school may influence their mathematical careers through college or, perhaps, for the rest of their lives. We have compiled this book to help you think about both the global and the particular issues that you will encounter as you begin your high school teaching experiences.

Questions and ideas regarding six major aspects of teaching are included in the discussions in this book. Section 1, "Professional Growth," emphasizes the importance of continuing your own professional development, both formally and informally. You will read suggestions for finding support from your colleagues and maintaining a balance between your personal and professional lives. Section 2, "Curriculum and Instruction," discusses the major components of planning and implementing instruction,

including ideas for using questioning strategies and student discussion to enhance mathematical thinking and methods for incorporating appropriate mathematical tools, such as technology, to support learning. Section 3, "Classroom Assessment," suggests assessment techniques to help you determine what your students understand and know. Section 4, "Classroom Management and Organization," includes helpful ideas for setting the direction of the class and organizing the learning environment. The articles in Section 5, "Equity," address important issues of diversity and equity that help you meet the needs of all your students. Finally, Section 6, "School and Community," supports you in dealing with both your school community and the larger community in which your students live, including suggestions for working with parents and colleagues.

Consider this book an interactive journal of ideas for you in your first years of teaching. As you read each section, consider how the ideas relate to your way of thinking and instructional approaches. Do they offer a potentially helpful variation to your own style? Are they consistent with your instructional philosophy? Use the journal space in each section to make notes on ideas that seem particularly useful to you, approaches you tried and how they worked for you, and modifications you made to the ideas suggested here. You will find that as your experience changes, your needs change; revisit this book several times during your first years of teaching to gain new perspectives on difficulties that you may experience.

The ideas discussed in this book are not meant to serve as a comprehensive list of classroom strategies or to espouse a particular instructional philosophy. Instead, they are presented to meet a number of more-open-ended goals: to launch your own thinking about a particular topic, such as assessment; to offer a quick solution to a pressing problem that you will have more time to analyze in the future; or to spur you to ask your colleagues specific questions, such as how to distribute and keep track of a classroom set of calculators. Moreover, the ideas and suggestions in this book highlight the complex and often overwhelming tasks that teachers must address. We hope this book will prompt you to seek out helpful colleagues and assist you in identifying useful resources and ideas to ensure that you thrive in your beginning years and develop into an effective teacher of high school mathematics.

1 SECTION

PROFESSIONAL GROWTH

Your first years of teaching will be challenging and rewarding—and stressful. You, as a new entrant to the profession, are expected to assume the same responsibilities as a twenty-year veteran, including everything from operating the copy machine to teaching reform-based curriculum. You may need to adapt and develop lessons, discover how to use new materials, determine the most effective classroom-management skills, and meet the needs of diverse students. As a teacher, you should continuously experiment with new methods and try to learn from your successes and mistakes. We should all strive to do so! As you face the realities of teaching, you may wonder where to turn to continue your professional growth. The following paragraphs suggest several novel resources for beginning the professional development that should take place throughout your career.

Self-Assessment

Reflecting on your own teaching is a vital step in your growth. Analyze your lessons, and think about what went well and what you might change. This reflection can lead to improved lesson planning and teaching practices. Keeping a journal is one way to record your reflections. Some questions to ponder include the following:

- What did I do in my lesson?
- What were the goals for my lesson?
- Did I accomplish my goals?
- What anticipated challenges did my students face during the lesson?
- What were some different ways of thinking that I observed as my students worked on a given task?
- How might I revise this lesson in the future?

Your Colleagues

Collaborating with fellow teachers is another way to grow professionally. Find colleagues who are knowledgeable and willing to share ideas that work. Of course, not all strategies that are effective for an experienced teacher will work for you. Be selective. Seek out new ideas and resources. Ask questions. And remember to share with others what works for you!

Support Groups

Many schools and districts offer formal induction programs and support groups for beginning teachers. Often groups of new teachers meet weekly or monthly to share common concerns and successes. Mentoring programs are also becoming more popular. Consider selecting and working with a mentor. Be willing to seek out more formal support groups. You do not have to face all your challenges alone!

Professional Journals and Organizations

Keep up with current practices and issues in education by reading professional journals. Find time each month to read one or two articles that interest you. Local, state, and national organizations hold annual meetings, academies, and workshops to help you grow professionally. Learn more about what conferences are offered in your area, and attend a conference or workshop to see how valuable such gatherings can be.

Coursework

You may have graduated only recently, but more coursework may be in your future. In the months to come, you might consider expanding your knowledge of mathematics content and pedagogy, as well as classroom practice, through some form of teacher education. Take time to investigate programs, and talk to others in your field about appropriate coursework for the topics in which you are interested.

Although this entire book is intended to provide support and ideas for your growth as a teacher of mathematics, this first section deals specifically with your professional growth. As you read the pages ahead, consider the following questions:

- How do I continue to develop my skills as a teacher to improve the abilities of my students?
- Where do I turn for feedback and advice on my teaching?
- How do I make my first year of teaching successful for me and for my students?

We believe that the habits of reflection you develop as you read this book and think about these questions will serve you well as you seek to achieve growth in your teaching career.

Four Crucial Insights for First-Year Teachers of Mathematics

Steve Leinwand

In light of the typical absence of collaborative mechanisms to "learn the ropes" of teaching—particularly the teaching of mathematics—I offer this set of four crucial insights for thriving as a beginning teacher. These insights are gleaned from extensive discussions with first- and second-year teachers and from the review of many professional performance portfolios. Moreover, they arise out of a desire to extend the "wisdom of practice" garnered by experienced teachers but shared too infrequently with those who are new to the profession.

Insight 1 Just because it worked once …

One of the most discouraging realities of teaching is that even though a certain approach worked first period, you have no guarantee that it will work fifth period. Conversely, just because something was a disaster this year or during your last-period class, you have no reason not to try it again next year or during a different period. The fact is that classroom dynamics and the distinctive personality of each student and class are often far more powerful determinants of the success or failure of a lesson than your plans. The excitement of teaching—even after years of practice—arises from the unique set of circumstances that you face every year with every new class and from the ongoing struggle to refine and modify your methods. This perspective helps you overcome the daily frustrations and the inevitable classes that "bomb."

Insight 2 Mistakes happen

Another aspect of teaching that is seldom discussed is how rare the "perfect class" is. In fact, you learn quickly that teaching a forty-five-minute class without making at least two mistakes is almost impossible. One mistake is usually a careless mathematical error made because you are thinking several steps ahead. Sometimes your students will catch the mistake, and sometimes the error sits on the chalkboard unnoticed until the classroom erupts in a disagreement about the final answer. The second mistake is usually pedagogical and results from calling on the wrong student at the wrong time or assigning the wrong problem at the wrong time. Either error is sure to engender confusion. When a supervisor or principal is in the room or when you are using technology, the likelihood of mistakes increases significantly. Once you realize that such mistakes are typical in all classes and almost inevitable during any given class, you can begin to shift your perspective and see most mistakes not as embarrassments but as welcome learning opportunities for both you and your students.

Insight 3 Do not try to work alone

The professional isolation of teachers is among the most serious impediments to improving practice and developing teaching skills. Unfortunately, most teachers practice their craft behind closed doors, minimally aware of what their colleagues are doing and usually unobserved and undersupported. Perpetuating this debilitating culture is irrational. Instead, you should realize that remedies for nearly every teaching obstacle reside among your colleagues if you are only willing to ask. As lonely as you may feel in your career, you are not alone. Through direct communication with colleagues, online interaction with other teachers, or the range of professional development opportunities offered locally and regionally, support and helpful suggestions are readily available.

Insight 4 If you do not occasionally feel inadequate, you are probably not doing the job

Just think about what you are being asked to do: teach in distinctly different ways from how you were taught mathematics; use hardware and software that did not exist a few years ago; make much more frequent use of group work; focus as much on problems, communication, and applications as on skills and procedures; teach groups of students that are far more heterogeneous than those of your predecessors; and assess understanding in more authentic ways. Feeling overwhelmed by this torrent of change is neither a weakness nor a lack of professionalism. It is an entirely rational response. A reasonable perspective is that an occasional sense of inadequacy is both inevitable and typical and should be channeled into stimulating the ongoing growth and learning that characterize the true professional.

Keep these insights in mind as you begin your career as a teacher; doing so may save you the sometimes-painful experience of learning them on your own.

Choosing and Working with a Mentor

Sharon Zagorski

New teachers continuously search for support, resources, and ideas during their first years in the profession to make sense of the realities of teaching. One important source of support, the use of mentor teachers, is becoming more prevalent both nationally and internationally. Finding and working with a mentor is a good idea for almost any new teacher. The following lists highlight important questions to consider when you are looking for someone to fulfill this role in your professional life.

What qualities should I look for in a mentor?

- A knowledgeable teacher who is committed to the profession

- A teacher who has a positive attitude toward the school, colleagues, and students and is willing to share his or her own struggles and frustrations, avoiding the naysayer who constantly complains in staff meetings

- A teacher who is accepting of beginning teachers, showing empathy and acceptance without judgment

- A teacher who continuously searches for better answers and more effective solutions to problems rather than believes that he or she already has the only right answer to every question and the best solution to every problem

- A teacher who leads and attends workshops and who reads or writes for professional journals

- An open, caring, and friendly individual who has good communication skills

- Someone who shares your teaching style, philosophy, grade level, or subject area

- A teacher who is following the path you want to follow, someone with whom you can relate and with whom you share mutual respect

- Someone who is aware of his or her own biases and opinions and encourages you to listen to advice but also to form your own opinions

What should I expect from an effective mentor?

- A mentor allows you to talk without interruptions and listens for your sake.

- A mentor maintains confidentiality in your discussions and interactions.

- A mentor helps you explore options, set goals, and attempt to do things your way, using your strengths and personality.

- A mentor builds on your strengths and avoids trying to transform you into a teacher clone using his or her style.

What are my responsibilities as a new teacher working with a mentor?

- Welcome the mentor's interest and concern.

- Realize that both partners can gain from the relationship.

- Realize that mutual respect, trust, and openness are the foundations for achieving success.

- Avoid a passive role; take the initiative in your own development by specifying your needs, soliciting feedback, and using the feedback without viewing it as criticism or an evaluation.

- Have realistic goals and expectations for what can be accomplished. Be open and sincere.

- Communicate any difficulties and concerns as clearly as possible. Be willing to discuss failures, as well as successes. Understand that learning comes from an examination of both.

- Follow through on commitments, and seek help when necessary. Asking for help is a sign not of weakness but of strength.

- Be honest with your mentor about important feelings. Contribute ideas and a variety of options for overcoming difficulties.

What are the benefits of having a mentor?

- Having a mentor gives you an opportunity to learn from an experienced teacher, who shares his or her personal knowledge, experiences, and insights.

- A mentor who helps you understand and cope with written and unwritten rules will ensure that you are quickly assimilated into the school culture.

- Working with a mentor gives you the chance to test ideas, strategies, and tactics in a friendly forum before you try them in a classroom.

- Having a mentor gives you access to coaching and counseling.

- A mentor can help you clarify your career goals by making you aware of local, state, and national professional organizations, thus opening the doors to continuing growth and development.

Your work with a mentor will be as rewarding and successful as you make it. This relationship should serve as a strong foundation for support and future professional growth.

Accepting or Requesting an Advanced Placement Class

Darren Pascavage

Early in your teaching career, you may have the opportunity to teach an Advanced Placement (AP) course. You may request the opportunity to teach such a course, or you may be asked to do so. Each scenario introduces issues to be considered, reconsidered, and re-reconsidered before you decide to accept the responsibility.

If you request to teach an AP course, be sure that you understand what you are getting into. To begin with, the workload is formidable: expect to spend at least twice as long preparing for a daily meeting of an AP course as you would for a daily meeting of a non-AP course, and be prepared to take home papers to be graded and reviewed every night and every weekend. Keep in mind that students, parents, and colleagues are likely to have high expectations for the course. Students usually know when a teacher is underprepared, confused, or insecure and may be dissatisfied and upset if you fail to meet their standards. Parents with high hopes for their children's success may wonder why homework is not graded nightly or why tests are not returned the day after they are taken. Parents have also been known to respond to the slightest hint of student discontent with concerned phone calls to department chairs or principals.

Furthermore, some parents and administrators will use your students' AP exam scores—fairly or unfairly—as a measure of your performance as a teacher. You may come to believe that your professional reputation rests on those scores, thereby only adding to the pressure that you place on yourself and your students. Indeed, all these factors combined can make your first AP experience feel burdensome, lonely, and thankless.

If you are asked to teach an AP course, you may wonder why you were chosen, especially if other qualified and more experienced teachers are available to accept such an assignment. Teachers who have more experience may not be interested in the subject or may be unwilling to devote time to additional planning, grading, preparation, and training. For this reason, the department chair or principal may have no other option but to come to you. Alternatively, you may be asked to teach an AP course because your more recent experiences in college have exposed you to new content, new pedagogy, and new uses of the technology that has become a focal point in both AP calculus and AP statistics.

My advice is to accept the responsibility of teaching an AP course only after you have demonstrated to yourself that you can handle the demands of your new career. In other words, if your student teaching experience left you feeling exhausted beyond all expectations or you were overwhelmed by the demands of your first year as a teacher, then you should probably wait at least a year or two before accepting the responsibility of an AP course. The chance to teach such a course may seem like a once-in-a-lifetime opportunity, but such opportunities have a way of coming around again—sometimes, more frequently than you might expect. If you are among those who meet the challenges of the first year of teaching with energy and enthusiasm to spare, then speak to your department chair or principal to express an interest in teaching an AP course.

If you are scheduled to teach an AP course, prepare yourself for the challenge by—

- taking advantage of as many in-service and summer training sessions as you can;

- becoming a part of the listserv appropriate to the course you teach, and participating often;

- speaking with colleagues, both in your school and at other schools, to gather ideas and discuss common concerns;

- reading professional journals regularly to stay up-to-date in the field; and

- making the extra time you need in your day to accommodate the AP workload; for example, negotiate a release from lunch, hall, or other monitoring duties

Provided that you do not neglect either your own needs—including food, water, and the occasional break from grading papers, reading professional material, and preparing for class—or the needs of your non-AP students, who also deserve your time and attention, you will soon find yourself thrilled at teaching secondary mathematics at the AP level.

Students' Perceptions of a Good Mathematics Teacher: Are Students and Teachers "on the Same Page"?

Joy B. Stallard
Denisse R. Thompson

In today's mathematics classroom, the role of the teacher is shifting from one who explains mathematics to one who guides students and facilitates their construction of their own mathematical understanding. Yet many high school students, particularly those who have not had NCTM Standards–based experiences in grades K–8, often view the best mathematics teacher as one who "gives clear, simple, and thorough explanations."

Roughly 1500 students taking a variety of courses were surveyed about their attitudes on a number of issues related to mathematics in school. These students were from four high schools in suburban, inner-city, rural, and small-town settings. Among the questions that the students were asked was the following:

What do you think are the good qualities of the best mathematics teacher you have ever had?

The students' responses foster insight into their perspectives on pedagogy. Among the most frequently cited qualities of good mathematics teachers were the following:

- Makes mathematics enjoyable or fun
- Makes mathematics interesting
- Does not move on to new material too quickly
- Gives clear, simple, and thorough explanations
- Helps students understand material
- Checks to make sure that students understand material

These responses suggest that students expect teachers to do most of the work to promote learning. Yet research suggests that learning is more successful when students construct it for themselves, that is, when they take more responsibility for their learning, in line with the recommendations of the NCTM *Standards* documents (1989, 2000). This dissonance between the profession's recommendations and students' expectations of the teacher's role can create unnecessary stress unless teachers are aware of the potential tension between these viewpoints. The differences in perspectives suggest that teachers need to explain or help students understand why pedagogical strategies other than "chalk and talk" are important in mathematics education. In other words, teachers need to enlist students as partners in fostering a learning community in the classroom. We encourage you to talk to your students and help them understand why the Standards-based strategies you use are important in helping them become mathematically successful.

I WISH I HAD KNOWN

TOP TEN THINGS I WISH I HAD KNOWN WHEN I STARTED TEACHING

Cynthia Thomas

10. Not every student will be interested every minute. No matter how much experience you have or how great you are at teaching, you will encounter times in the classroom when no student is interested! The solution is to change your tone of voice, move around the room, or switch from lecturing to some other activity. Maybe you can even use a manipulative to increase the students' understanding and, possibly, their level of interest.

9. If a lesson is going badly, stop. Even if you have planned a lesson and have a clear goal in mind, if your approach is not working—for whatever reason—stop! Regroup and start over with a different approach, or abandon your planned lesson entirely and go on to something else. At the end of the day, be honest with yourself as you examine what went wrong and make plans for the next day.

8. Teaching will get easier. Maybe not tomorrow or even next week, but at some point in the year, your job *will* get easier! Try to remember your first day in the classroom. Were you nervous? Of course; all of us were. See how much better you are as a teacher already? By next year, you will be able to look back on today and be amazed at how much you have learned and how much easier so many aspects of teaching are!

7. You do not have to volunteer for everything. Do not feel that you always have to say yes each time you are asked to participate. Know your limits. Practice saying, "Thank you for thinking of me, but I do not have the time to do a good job with another task right now." Of course, you must accept your responsibility as a professional and do your fair share, but remember to be realistic about your limits.

6. Not every student or parent will love you. And you will not love every one of them, either! Those feelings are perfectly acceptable. We teachers are not hired to love students and their parents; our job is to teach students and, at times, their parents as well. Students do not need a friend who is your age; they need a facilitator, a guide, a role model for learning.

Above all else, remember: "Those who can, teach. Those who cannot, do something far less important!"

5. You cannot be creative in every lesson. In your career, you *will* be creative, but for those subjects that do not inspire you, you can turn to other resources for help. Textbooks, teaching guides, and professional organizations, such as NCTM, are designed to support you in generating well-developed lessons for use in the classroom. When you do feel creative and come up with an effective and enjoyable lesson, be sure to share your ideas with other teachers, both veterans and newcomers to the profession.

4. *No one* can manage portfolios, projects, journals, creative writing, and student self-assessment all at the same time and stay sane! The task of assessing all these assignments is totally unreasonable to expect of yourself as a beginning teacher. If you want to incorporate these types of exercises into your teaching, pick one for this year and make it a priority in your classroom. Then, next year or even the year after that, when you are comfortable with the one extra assignment you picked, you can incorporate another innovation into your teaching.

3. Some days you will cry, but the good news is, some days you will laugh! Learn to laugh *with* your students and *at* yourself!

2. You will make mistakes. You cannot undo your mistakes, but berating yourself for them is counterproductive. If the mistake requires an apology, make it and move on. No one is keeping score.

1. This *is* the best job on earth! Stand up straight! Hold your head high! Look people in the eye and proudly announce, "I am a teacher!"

Keeping a Professional Journal

Susan Kyle Arn

As you begin teaching, keep a good professional journal. Once a month, update this journal by noting any professional development meetings you have attended, presentations you have made, professional organizations you have joined, and so on. With the journal, keep any certificates of attendance or completion you have earned and a copy of your transcripts, along with a copy of your evaluation and your current teaching certificate. You may also want to include articles from the newspaper or professional journals that you value or notes on topics of interest in your career. After a few years of teaching, you will need to create a new journal, but remember to keep the old one.

You will be surprised how much you will add to your journal each month. It will also come in handy when you need to update your resume or you begin to apply for awards and grants. This journal will become one of the most important professional references that you have.

I NEVER LEARNED

SEVEN THINGS I NEVER LEARNED IN METHODS CLASS

Margaret R. Meyer

1. Do not think that students never notice what clothes you wear or when you last cut your hair. They are quite observant about such things because these concerns are very important in their own lives. When building a professional wardrobe, do make the choice of comfort over fashion, especially when you are buying shoes.

2. Do not bore your friends with school stories unless they are teachers, too. A story that is funny to a teacher is often not funny to those in other occupations. Do try to balance your life with friends who work outside of education.

3. Do not take your health for granted when working with children. Keep a box of tissues on your desk, and insist that students use them. Ask students to bring in replacement boxes from home; they are usually happy to do so. Wash your hands frequently.

4. Do not think you will always be twenty-something. Pay attention to saving for your retirement. Take advantage of tax-sheltered savings plans.

5. Do not take too long to recover from your undergraduate degree. Start a graduate program as soon as possible. Doing so will pay off well in the long run.

6. Do not isolate yourself behind your closed door. Find colleagues with whom you can talk, plan, share successes and failures, and continue to grow professionally.

7. Do not ever tell your students how old you are, especially when they ask you directly. Instead, add at least thirty years to your age when answering because that age is how old they really think you are. Do think about retiring when your answer starts to sound believable.

Remember—Write It Down!

A great way to keep track of plans that did not go well, lessons that took too much time, or specific ideas or exercises that drove a lesson home is by writing them directly on your lesson script. Recalling a good teaching suggestion from a previous year may be difficult unless you take the time to jot it down where you are sure to see it when it is needed.

—Barbara A. Burns

Keeping a Proper Perspective about Your Students

Duane A. Cooper

One of the greatest professional lessons I ever learned was from a student named Ollie Gary*. This student did everything imaginable to be disruptive and to get under my skin, and he succeeded. I love children—and mathematics—but at the time, I hated Ollie Gary. Other children's misbehavior seemed to be youthful mischief or bravado, but to me, Ollie's antics were mean-spirited and intolerable. After one particularly trying day, I was fuming over something Ollie had done. Then I had a revelation: I taught twenty-nine students who adored me and frequently made their feelings evident; I was crazy to let the one remaining child irritate me. For the rest of the year, Ollie Gary never upset me again. Oh, he tried, but I was able to dismiss his annoying behavior. My resolution to tie my emotions to the many appreciative students I teach remains valuable to me; quite often, I have "that one student" in a class who is difficult in some way, yet I cope.

I have no greater joy in my life than teaching mathematics. My wish for beginning mathematics teachers is that you find the same delight and passion that I find in my teaching. I have three pieces of advice for you: Love the mathematics, love the children, and never let one student get you down.

---

* A pseudonym

Notes:

CURRICULUM AND INSTRUCTION

Teaching involves many decisions, most of which must be made before a lesson begins. These decisions give teachers an opportunity to reflect on the kinds of learning experiences they intend for their students. As a teacher, you may find yourself deciding such issues as what topic should be the focus of a lesson, how to engage students in that topic, what questions to ask students, how to guide discussions to both encourage participation and advance particular mathematical ideas, and what tools or resources to use. These decisions are important because they influence the kinds of learning opportunities and views of mathematics that your students will have. In this section, you will find ideas to guide you as you contemplate these questions.

This section has three major themes: (1) Planning, (2) Questioning and Discourse, and (3) Instructional Tools and Resources. The themes reflect multiple and mostly distinct facets of the complex decision-making you will face as a teacher. As you design and carry out your instructional plans, you will need to consider and reflect on all three areas to teach mathematics for understanding.

Planning

Most likely, planning will occupy a major portion of your time during your beginning years of teaching. To carry out the day-to-day functions of teaching and to be effective in your eyes and in the eyes of your colleagues and administrators, you must understand the scope and nature of the curriculum that you are teaching and the best methods for implementing that curriculum. Planning requires that you consider both the short-term view—what you plan to accomplish in a given lesson—and the long-term view—what should be the lasting learning outcomes of your teaching, such as instilling a mathematical disposition and an ability to solve problems in your students. In this section, you will find guidance to assist you in planning, including how to determine what you are responsible for teaching, what classroom policies are appropriate and effective, and what instructional strategies to use.

Questions and Discourse

As a teacher, you serve as the representative of the larger academic and mathematical communities, and you control the flow of information to your students and the depth to which they think about mathematical ideas. One important component that defines your role is the kinds of questions you ask students during instruction. These questions can serve to assess students' knowledge and to initiate students into mathematical discussions. Because different forms of questions serve distinct purposes, you will need to consider and balance your short-term and long-term goals in determining whether to ask a question that requires a brief factual response or one that requires an extended response in which students must explain their thinking. Reading this section will help you determine the types of questions to ask, both in planning your lesson and in conducting it with your students.

Instructional Tools and Resources

While planning your lessons, you will need to identify what tools and resources, such as technology and manipulatives, to incorporate and how best to use them. For example, you may need a system for distributing and accounting for manipulatives and calculators or advice on how to design lessons that include the use of computer software. Lessons that integrate calculators, computers, and manipulatives may require a good deal of time; however, such lessons tend to offer different avenues through which students can engage in mathematics. As a beginning teacher, you may want to implement tools and resources gradually as you learn how their use can enhance your students' mathematical understanding.

ABCs for Teachers: Answers to Beginning Concerns

Gladis Kersaint
Edward Mooney

As a new teacher, you have many new challenges ahead of you—students to get to know; school and district policies to learn and implement; and undoubtedly, questions to answer about teaching, learning, and assessing mathematics. To help you meet these challenges, here are a few responses to "frequently asked questions" posed by beginning and change-of-career teachers.

What am I responsible for teaching?

Not all beginning or change-of-career teachers are given copies of the mathematics curriculum guide or framework that they are responsible for teaching. Often, teachers are simply handed the textbooks that are being used for the courses they will teach. If you do not have a copy of the curriculum guide or framework for your courses, request one from the principal or appropriate school staff member. Typically, your state's department of education will outline the mathematics curriculum; however, your school district may have developed its own curriculum that fits the state's guidelines. Many states now have their curriculum frameworks available online.

How much of the curriculum will I be expected to teach? How will I cover everything?

Most likely, teaching the required curriculum is feasible, but you will need to put the task into perspective. First, review the curriculum and the textbook. Look at the extensive list of topics that you are to teach. Ask yourself, "Can any of these topics be combined through the use of appropriate instructional strategies or learning experiences?" You may be able to identify a number of creative ways to integrate various topics. With few exceptions, most conventional textbooks should be considered resources for instruction, not the sole basis for instruction.

Having reviewed your curriculum, you will be better prepared to decide when using other resources may be more appropriate.

What should I emphasize when I teach?

What you emphasize will depend on your teaching philosophy and that of your school or district. If you have not done so already, begin to develop a philosophy about what you expect your students to gain from your mathematics instruction. Proceed from those ideas by focusing on the topics that you believe are important. When you know what you want to accomplish in your classroom, determining whether you are reaching your goals will be easier. Compare the importance of completing pages of drill exercises with helping students develop or expand their reasoning skills. With emerging technologies, the focus on procedures alone has become less important. Students need to understand mathematical concepts, know when and how to apply them, and know how to extend and justify their mathematical ideas.

How do I get my students to cooperate?

Students today are quite savvy and seldom accept actions without appropriate rationales. Talk to your students about what you are trying to achieve in the classroom, and why. Students will know what to expect when they are informed about and understand your goals for them. They must find that the reasons you provide match the concerns that are important to them. This awareness will help students interpret the interactions they experience in your classroom.

Depending on their experiences in other mathematics classrooms, students may initially resist any approach that differs from the norm. The good news is that with time, fortitude, and conviction on your part, students can learn to appreciate their newly developed skills or the strategies that you are encouraging.

How much homework should I assign?

Assign as much homework as necessary to augment your instruction. That is, decide what you expect from the homework. What information will it provide you? Can you get the same information by assigning only five problems instead of fifty?

As a new teacher, you may easily find yourself falling into "survival mode," in which you become so fixated on the day-to-day occurrences in the classroom that you neglect long-term planning. If you begin with the overall goal in mind, then you can prepare more effectively for the opportunities and challenges that lie ahead.

Questions to Ask While Planning an Engaging Mathematics Lesson

Margaret McIntosh
Roni Jo Draper

Lessons that are dull to students are difficult to pull off; and lessons that are dull to teachers are impossible to pull off. To keep your instruction varied and fresh, ask yourself the following questions as you prepare your lessons:

How can this lesson be a game?

Students enjoy games, and sometimes just the act of playing a game energizes the class. Popular games, such as Pictionary, relay races, bingo, Jeopardy, Wheel of Fortune or hangman, and Concentration, can often be modified for use in the classroom.

How many different ways can this information be presented?

Students benefit from repetition, especially if the repetition comes in a variety of forms. Look for multiple ways to present and reinforce the topic at hand.

What novel activity could accompany this lesson?

Novel activities, such as projects, give students opportunities to apply their knowledge. Projects can also motivate students to want to learn.

How can students get a multisensory experience with this lesson?

Mathematics instruction should include all the senses—touch, sight, hearing, smell, and taste. For example, when students use orange peels to demonstrate that the surface area of a sphere is four times the area of one great circle of the sphere, they will not forget the concept or the experience.

What can students write about?

Many forms of writing can be used in the classroom to accomplish different purposes. For example, students can take notes using words, numbers, diagrams, symbols, or pictures—whatever means works for them. Learning logs give students the opportunity to do a small amount of writing in a short period of time. Students can also engage in longer writing assignments, such as composing essays, creative stories or problems, poetry, or children's books.

What kind of connections can be made?

Always seek ways to make connections among various topics in mathematics. For example, algebra can be applied to probability just as easily as it can be applied to problems in percents. You may also look for ways to make connections between topics in mathematics and other disciplines. For example, using the metric system, computing percent error, and graphing and interpreting data are frequently required in science and social studies.

What reading assignment could enhance this lesson?

Research indicates that when students are given two passages to read on the same topic, they show better comprehension of the second passage and remember more about it. Even children's books may be useful when you are looking for reading material to reinforce students' learning.

Patchwork Mathematics: Empowering Mathematics Teachers through Children's Literature

Charlene E. Beckmann
Denisse R. Thompson
Richard A. Austin

Students enjoy literature and are surprised and intrigued when they discover that a piece of literature has a mathematical interpretation. When used in conjunction with mathematics textbooks, children's literature can help lift mathematics off the page and into real or fantasy life, engaging students at a high level. In addition, literature helps teachers integrate mathematics across several content areas. For example, children's books about patchwork quilts, such as *Eight Hands Round* and *The Seasons Sewn*, both by Ann Whitford Paul (1991, 1996), can provide a context for a number of mathematical explorations. The books have explicit ties to social studies and early American art, describing the importance of patchwork quilts to early Americans and the origins of several illustrated quilt blocks.

Students can study fractions by sketching a quilt block of their choice on graph paper and determining the fractional part of each of the colors that makes up a single block. They can also use quilt blocks to study functions by examining a table containing the number of pieces of each shape and color needed to make one, two, three, or any number *n* copies of a specific quilt block. Some intricate quilt blocks can be used to study slope, ratio, angle measures, and tessellations.

Many other books also have strong mathematical ties. Ask your students about the books they are reading in other classes and for recreation, or wander through the children's section of a library or bookstore with mathematics in mind. Other concepts that readily arise from children's stories include ratio and proportion (e.g., *Jim and the Beanstalk* [Briggs 1970], *Counting on Frank* [Clement 1991]), patterns and functions (e.g., *The Very Hungry Caterpillar* [Carle 1969], or any counting book), geometry (any shape book or books on architecture), and rates and linear functions (any book comparing speeds of animals or humans). The list is endless. Happy hunting!

Small Groups in My Classroom?

Art Johnson

A number of studies have suggested that using small groups can improve students' learning in mathematics. *Principles and Standards for School Mathematics* (NCTM 2000) notes that small groups enable students to try out their ideas before presenting them to the entire class. Much has been written about the benefits of working in small groups—for example, students can learn from one another, and explorations can be more diverse. Much has also been written about the pitfalls—for example, assessment may be difficult, one student may do all the work, and students may not spend adequate time on task. Still,

many questions remain, especially about the use of small groups in the upper grades. When should teachers use small groups? What types of topics or activities can be enhanced in a small-group setting? Given that high-stakes tests loom at the end of the year, how can small groups fit into a crowded syllabus? What is a good way to manage a classroom of small groups?

The small-group setting can be an effective format to promote mathematics learning with many activities. The activities listed below are common to most mathematics classes and fit easily into a standard course syllabus. Using small groups for these activities does not require additional time, special topics, or extensive preparation. The suggestions below are a representative list of possibilities for using groups at all grade levels.

Data Gathering

Students often gather experimental data in class for analysis. When students work in small groups and pool their results, they are able to make conjectures on the basis of their data. Small-group data may also be combined to compare large-group results and to draw inferences. Some specific tasks that benefit from gathering and analyzing data in this way include explorations involving computer-based laboratory technology, investigations with interactive geometry software, or analysis of data from probability experiments, such as flipping coins. Students might also collect data outside the classroom, for example, from the Internet or student surveys. They might gather personal information, such as the time needed for each student in the class to travel from home to school or the size of each student's bedroom. This information can be compared or combined with the data of others in the group to make a conjecture or to construct a data display.

Explorations

Students might work together in small groups to develop conjectures about how the graph of an equation changes as various parameters of the equation are altered. Small groups might explore the area and side lengths of similar figures to discover the relationship between linear and area measures. In both tasks, students can examine their findings in small groups to produce effective conjectures.

(Continued on page 18)

Small Groups in My Classroom?
(Continued from page 17)

Projects

Small-group projects can be beneficial activities for extending or deepening students' mathematics knowledge. Small groups of students can effectively report to the class about such topics as various types of geometries, consumer affairs, or real-world applications.

Open-ended Problems

Students can explore many open-ended problems in small-group settings. For example, the box problem requires students to determine the best way to cut out corner squares from a sheet of paper so that it will fold up to form the box with the largest volume. This problem, as well as those involving maximum-minimum points, promotes interesting discussions as students form conclusions on the basis of their results.

Review Sessions

Small-group settings can be effective for students who are reviewing material in preparation for major tests in the course or for standardized tests. Students work together to recall, clarify, and extend their knowledge of the course material.

Group Tests

Students may also be assessed in small-group settings. For example, students might be given a single copy of a test with the requirement that no erasures or changes may be made to answers once they are recorded on the test paper. Alternatively, small groups of students may be given a few minutes to discuss the entire test; then each group member takes the test individually. A third option is to distribute different portions of the test to individual group members, then combine their results for a single group score.

Outdoor Tasks

Students benefit more from outside activities or explorations when they work in small groups. For example, students might search the school for examples of the golden rectangle. A small group is also the best setting for using geometry skills to measure the height of a flagpole indirectly or to find the angle of elevation of the sun.

After you have selected activities for small groups, you must consider small-group management. The logistics of setting up small groups can be problematic if left to chance. Small groups seem to function best if the group is composed of four members. This size is large enough to allow for meaningful discussion among group members but not so large that the group is unwieldy or has difficulty staying on task. Further, groups of four can easily be divided into pairs for some explorations.

The composition of a group is another important consideration. Groups in a classroom should be balanced according to ability and ethnicity. Early in the year, a balance of personalities is valuable, but this need should diminish in importance as the year progresses and students work in class together. Groups should be changed every two or three weeks to give students the opportunity to work with everyone in the class.

Establishing clear goals for small groups is essential. At the start of the year, you may need to assign specific roles to group members, such as reporter, recorder, materials manager, and so forth. Describing and even role-playing the various responsibilities of each group member may be helpful. Your assessment of small-group work might emphasize not only the final product of the group but also the involvement of each group member. That is, how well did each member contribute to the group effort? Was each member prepared, engaged, and active? Assessing the process, as well as the product, can help ensure that all members of the group offer valuable input to the group's tasks.

A productive group session does not happen simply by having students push their desks together to work on a problem. Successful groups require careful planning, from the activities and the group composition to the responsibilities of the students and appropriate assessments. But the result is worth the effort. All levels of students can benefit from participating in small groups as a regular feature of their mathematics classroom experience.

Making Group Work Effective in the Mathematics Classroom

Abbe H. Herzig
David T. S. Kung

Group work, sometimes called *cooperative or collaborative learning*, has numerous benefits for your students, including—

- enhancing their understanding,

- developing their problem-solving skills through work on complex tasks,

- increasing their appreciation of diversity among their peers, and

- improving their communication and social skills.

By struggling with challenging concepts with their peers, conducting brainstorming sessions, explaining their understandings and misunderstandings, and communicating about their problem-solving strategies, students deepen their understanding of difficult mathematical concepts. Group work also affords you the opportunity to see what your students do and do not understand and to learn about their mathematical thinking and problem-solving strategies—information you can use to help plan your instruction.

Selecting group-work tasks

Group work involves more than just putting students' desks side by side and assigning them to work together. The tasks you give your students should be complex enough to require them to cooperate while providing roles for the group members to ensure that each student remains engaged in the work of the group. That is, you want to promote the students' interdependence for the work of the group and each student's individual accountability for his or her learning.

Instead of giving students worksheets of problems to solve, give them complex problems that require them to engage in brainstorming and problem solving together. Avoid tasks that allow students to divide up the project into parts and work individually.

Group composition

Teachers and parents sometimes become concerned that the weaker students in a group will rely on the work of the stronger ones, but remember that the laziest students are not necessarily the weakest ones. "Freeloading" can be avoided with the appropriate selection of tasks that require the input of all students; remember to design tasks that engage all students and hold them all accountable for the group's results. You might try rearranging the groups to place students who are not doing their share in a group together. With no one else to depend on, they may have to get to work.

The teacher's role

No single teaching technique is effective in all circumstances, but group work should play a prominent role in mathematics instruction. To determine what works best for your students, you may want to use a variety of strategies, adapting these guidelines to the individuals in your classroom. Keep in mind, too, that your job is not finished after you have planned and launched a small-group session; be sure to interact regularly with the groups and observe them as they work. By circulating through the classroom and sitting with each group for a while, you can see which strategies are useful and which are not and adjust the groups or the tasks accordingly.

TAP INTO MAGIC

Tap into the Magic of Your Students

Claudia Bertolone-Smith

Here are some ideas on how to find magic in your mathematics teaching:

- Know how each lesson fits into the bigger picture of what you are teaching. For example, if you are teaching a unit about multiplication, each lesson should somehow tie into that goal. Remind and show students how each lesson is related to multiplication.

- Be prepared for the students who will understand a topic right away and those who will need extra help. "I'm done" and "I don't get it" are both valid states of mind when learning mathematics. Make sure that you acknowledge and honor each intellectual state in your classroom, and know how you will help students move on meaningfully.

- If you want magic in your lessons, here is where to find it: in your students. Inside each of them is a curious, investigative, patterning, sorting, and classifying mind. Include them. Ask them what they think. Ask them what they see. Ask them to share their ideas, opinions, and reactions.

A "MUST-DO" LIST

A "Must-Do" List for Planning

Jane Till-Schröder

- Start each day with a quick problem to engage students the moment they walk into the classroom. Give a short quiz that directly relates to the last class. Students get in the habit of reviewing their notes before they come to class, a practice they might never engage in otherwise.

- Always plan to give an assignment. First-year teachers tend to move through the material more slowly because they want to teach their subject thoroughly. Move on! Students are capable of much more understanding than we ever give them credit for.

- Finally, know your curriculum. Make sure that the learning taking place inside your classroom coincides with what is going on in similar classrooms across the country.

TIPS FOR SUCCESS

Tips for a Successful First Year

Agnes M. Rash

- Be selective in assigning homework.
- Plan your homework so that students can complete it in thirty to forty-five minutes.
- Remember that overburdening students with excessive homework may result in students' not trying to do the work at all.

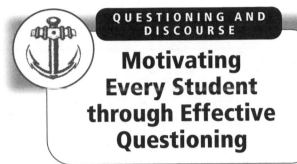

QUESTIONING AND DISCOURSE

Motivating Every Student through Effective Questioning

Jane M. Wilburne

Experienced teachers know that good, motivating questions can help keep students on task, prompt them to think about the material, and give them opportunities to reflect on their understanding of the lesson. Effective questioning engages all students, not just one or two in the class.

To be effective, questioning in the classroom should be used as both an instructional strategy and an assessment strategy. For students, the questions posed by the teacher should enhance their learning and encourage them to become involved in the lesson. For teachers, the questions posed should enable her or his assessment of the students' understanding of the material and the effectiveness of the lesson. If students appear confused and have no sense of how to answer the questions, the teacher should make the appropriate adjustments to be sure that each student understands.

Effective questioning should engage students in an exploration of the material. Questioning should require students to use critical-thinking skills, not simply to give rote answers. Students should be engaged in the learning and challenged by the questioning, and they should assume much of the responsibility for the discussions and explanations that take place in the classroom.

You should prepare high-quality questions at the same time that you plan your lessons. Giving some thought to the questions you will pose helps guide the lesson through an appropriate sequence of activities and keeps you and the students on task.

Keep the summary in table 1 (Wilburne) (p. 22) on your desk to remind you of various questioning techniques of effective teachers, but do not feel that you must master all these techniques in one lesson. Strive to incorporate one technique into your questioning each week. Effective questioning takes time and practice. Keep an index card on which you list various questioning techniques that seemed to work well and those that did not work well.

Take time to reflect on how effective your questions were during your lessons. Did they motivate the students? Did they promote curiosity? Did they inspire the students to want to learn more? As you refine your questioning techniques, you will discover that you, too, learn from each question you pose.

A Short Story for Mathematics Teachers

John E. Hammett III

During the review of assigned homework problems, Jason volunteers his answer to the following question: "What is the area of a rectangular garden with dimensions 6 feet by 4 feet?" Jason says with some pride, "20 feet." His teacher begins to respond but then abruptly pauses.

Remembering some good advice about listening carefully to what students say and taking a deep breath, Jason's teacher asks him, "How did you get your answer?" The student explains that he doubled the length, resulting in 12; then he doubled the width, resulting in 8; he then added these two numbers to get the area.

Before saying that Jason is wrong, the teacher hesitates once again. An almost-imperceptible-yet-knowing smile forms on the teacher's face. "Jason, that's a correct answer to a good question, but it is not the question being asked in this problem. What question did you actually answer, Jason?" The student wrinkles his eyebrows in response to the teacher's comment and subsequent question, looking slightly puzzled. Opening the conversation to the rest of the class, the teacher asks, "What problem did Jason solve?" Melissa raises her hand; when the teacher calls on her, she says, "He found the distance around the rectangular garden. That's the perimeter."

The teacher thanks Melissa for her contribution and returns to Jason to verify his understanding. Jason nods in agreement. He takes a quick look at the diagram of the rectangular garden that he drew in his notebook and asks, "Is the correct answer 24 square feet?" The teacher again asks him to explain his answer, and he does. This time, Jason says that he multiplied the rectangle's two dimen-

(Continued on page 23)

TABLE 1 (WILBURNE). *Summary of Questioning Techniques*

Ineffective Questioning Techniques	Effective Questioning Techniques
Asking yes/no questions	Asking questions that require short responses in which students must justify their answers, for example, • "How did you know that answer?" • "Can you explain how you found that solution?" • "How can we figure this problem out?"
Calling out a student's name, then asking the question	Posing a question to the whole class, then pausing—for a long period of time if necessary. After the pause, try one of these tactics: • Have students answer the question in their notebooks before you call on someone. • Have students discuss their answers with partners before you call on one or two students. • Inform students that you are going to call on two or three of them, but first, they must all think about the question.
Asking questions that are vague or misleading	Stating questions that are clear and target the learning goals
Answering your own question if no one in the class responds	Requiring students to work in pairs to discuss the question or write down their answers in their notebooks and share their solutions with partners
Asking, "Do you have any questions? Does everybody understand?"	Phrasing questions to determine whether the students understand, for example, • "Who can ask the class a question about the lesson?" • "Each of you should write down one question you have about the lesson. Then, ask your partner." • "Did anyone come up with a question that his or her partner was unable to answer?"
Asking teacher-centered questions, such as, "Can someone explain to me…?"	Asking questions for the class, such as, "Can someone explain to us…?"
Asking questions that require the class as a whole to chant a response; for example, "Everyone, what kind of angle is this?"	Asking questions to help identify which students may not understand; for example, "Identify this type of angle in your notebook. When you are done, look up."
Asking only a few students questions throughout the period	Calling on as many students as possible
Informing a student that his or her answer is wrong	Guiding students through a series of questions to realize their errors
Asking the same type of questions over and over again	Asking a variety of questions in a variety of ways
Talking in a monotone voice	Getting excited and using inflection in your voice; whispering occasionally for effect like you have a big secret
Standing in the same location when asking questions	Moving around the room to make students aware that they are all involved in the lesson
Praising students who answer with a blunt "good"	Using pauses! After a student answers, ask other students what they think, for example, "Do you agree with his answer, Mary? What do you think, John?"

A Short Story for Mathematics Teachers
(Continued from page 21)

sions to find the area of the garden. When the teacher asks, "Is this the correct answer to this question?" Jason replies with confidence, "Yes!"

As the class discussion expands to include additional homework problems and other students, the teacher real-izes that this incident should have a positive impact on how Jason learns mathematics. By listening to the student's solution, the teacher, as well as Jason's classmate, Melissa, helped him correct his own misconception, thereby foster-ing success and self-confidence instead of failure and self-doubt. And Jason, Melissa, and the other students in the class competently and confidently calculated rectangular areas happily ever after.

The Teacher's Questions and Students' Learning:
Issues to Consider

Azita Manouchehri

One of the most striking aspects of teaching is that the teacher's speech consists largely of questions. These questions are central to the type of learning that takes place in the classroom. Naturally, questions are built around varying forms of thinking. Some questions are aimed at recall of information, whereas others promote problem solving. In a general sense, teachers' questions control students' learning because they focus students' attention on specific features of the concepts they learn. Moreover, these questions establish and validate students' perceptions about what is important to know to be suc-cessful in mathematics class.

Traditionally, teachers' questions tended to have a narrow focus, measuring solely students' mastery of algo-rithms. However, with the current emphasis on processes in mathematics and the expectation that students will develop conceptual understanding of mathematical ideas, teachers need to learn to ask questions that give learners opportunities to communicate their thoughts, develop their reasoning ability, and increase their depth of under-standing. With their questions, teachers can gather detailed data on how students think and what they actu-ally know. In this light, an integral aspect of effective instructional planning is determining what questions to pose in class. Asking good questions is a sophisticated skill that requires practice; thoughtful planning; and reflec-tion on, and analysis of, both the mathematical and the pedagogical goals of lessons.

The form of a question determines the type of answer that a teacher obtains from her or his students. A question can be posed in a *closed form,* soliciting dichoto-mous right-wrong or true-false answers from students. In contrast, questions posed in *open form,* such as *how* or *why* questions, elicit descriptions of a certain type, either a solution strategy or a process through which the stu-dents reached some answer. Consider, for instance, the following pairs of questions:

- "Does everyone understand the method of elimina-tion?" versus "When is the use of the elimination method in solving systems of linear equations more advantageous than other methods?"
- "Are you clear on the difference between the meth-ods of elimination and substitution?" versus "What should you consider when deciding which method to use when solving problems that involve systems of linear equations? How do you decide which method is more efficient?"
- "What is the next step?" versus "What could we do next, and why? How could we proceed from here?"
- "Solve the following system of linear equations" ver-sus "Write a system of linear equations for which the solution is point (4, 5)."
- "Is this statement true or false?" versus "When is this statement true, and when is it false? How do you know?"
- "Does anyone have any questions about what we did?" versus "What are some good questions to ask about what we discussed today?"
- "Is this process clear to everyone?" versus "Identify three features of this process that are clearest to you."

Although each question form is useful, depending on spe-cific teacher objectives, these examples clearly show that the two categories of questions elicit different types of information from students. Each question form prompts students to engage in a different kind of thinking about the mathematics content they study, but the open ques-tions force them to think more deeply.

Using Learning Logs in the Mathematics Classroom

Roni Jo Draper
Margaret E. McIntosh

Learning logs provide space for students to respond to writing prompts. Our use of learning logs has allowed us to know our students better, to understand their thinking better, to communicate individually with students through the written word, and to reevaluate our instruction on the basis of students' responses. The types and uses of learning logs can vary widely; what follows is a partial list of applications for learning logs in the mathematics classroom.

- Learning logs can be used to open a lesson, readying students for the topic and allowing the teacher to assess students' knowledge of material that is to be presented. Sample prompts might include "What do you already know about slope [or another concept]?" "What do you think you might learn today about slope?" "What do you need to learn about slope?"

- Learning logs can also be used to conclude a lesson, helping students reflect on what they have learned and identify gaps in their understanding after instruction. Sample prompts might include "What did you learn about slope [or another concept] today?" "What questions do you still have about slope after today's lesson?" "How does what you learned today about slope fit with what you already knew about slope?"

- Learning logs compel students to articulate their thinking. The following writing prompts can shed light on how well students understand mathematical concepts: "Choose the hardest problem from today's assignment, and explain how you solved it." "Find the error in the following problem, and explain how to solve this problem without an error." "Solve the following problem in two different ways, and explain why both ways work."

- The following prompts can help teachers evaluate their students' attitudes and biases: "How do you feel about mathematics?" "Why are you taking this class?" "Describe the ideal mathematics class."

- Finally, these prompts can help students reflect on their study strategies and skills: "What do you do when you get stuck on a homework problem?" "How do you take notes for this class, and what do you do with the notes after class?" "How do you prepare for tests and quizzes?"

Students can use about five minutes at the beginning or end of class to respond to prompts, thereby allowing the teacher to read and reply to students' writing quickly. Here are some more hints for using learning logs in the mathematics classroom:

- Use learning logs frequently, at least several times a week.

- Do not accept partial, ill-conceived, or no-effort answers; simply have students rewrite their responses until they have met the standard.

- Respond to students' writing, even briefly, to make sure students know that their learning logs are being read.

Tip for a Successful First Year: Silence Is Golden!

Silence is golden! When you pose a question, give students time to think about their answers before rephrasing the question.

—*Agnes M. Rash*

Something I Never Learned in Methods Class: Know Your Students

Do not expect every student to be as excited about mathematics as you are. Some students will share your enthusiasm, but many will not. Get to know what outside interests your students have. Find out what things they excel at, and celebrate those accomplishments with them. Consider how these areas could be used in contexts for mathematics.

—*Margaret R. Meyer*

TOOLS

Mathematics Learning with Technology

Ed Dickey
Melina Deligiannidou
Ashley Lanning

The purpose of using technology is not to make the learning of mathematics easier, but richer and better.

—Alfinio Flores

The first axiom in technology planning is, Let the mathematics drive the lesson. Look for ideas that allow you to use technology to enhance your students' understanding of the mathematics they are learning. Avoid teaching technology for the sake of technology. Try to attend an NCTM or a state mathematics conference; both abound with sessions in which experienced teachers explain and demonstrate how they use technology with their students.

Remember to start small but to *start*. If you incorporate technology just once a semester in each class you teach, you are making progress. By adding one more technology lesson each semester, you can, within five to ten years, become an exemplary technology-using teacher.

Students often need orientation to the activity you have planned. Realize that once they are working with the computer, they will no longer be paying attention to you. Technology removes the locus of control from the teacher to the computer, calculator, or group of students using the technology. Plan your lesson in phases. You might begin with an introduction to the whole class. Explain the specific task for students to accomplish or the problem you wish to have them solve. For some activities, you may be wise to pose the problem in vague terms to allow your students a wide range of options, but keep in mind that some students need more structure or direction. A well-constructed worksheet with specific questions can scaffold an otherwise unproductive investigation.

Your role with technology is that of a coach. Resist having students work individually. Working in groups minimizes the number of questions you have to answer and allows students to help one another. Provide opportunities for students to share their work with the whole class.

This activity allows you to view their presentations from the sidelines and think about the mathematics instead of what you plan to say next.

Using technology as part of student assessment is a matter of consistency; after all, if you believe that technology enhances learning, then it will also augment assessment. Further, using technology increases the authenticity of assessment, making it more relevant to the world of the student. Performance tasks offer an effective method for using technology in assessment.

Regardless of what software you use, students need time and assistance to learn the application. Often, the more powerful the software, the more effort required to learn to use it. Spreadsheet, interactive geometry, and computer algebra system (CAS) software require students to apply themselves to work effectively. Calculators require orientation. Invest class time to ensure that your students develop useful technology skills. This investment will pay off with enhanced learning of both the technology and the mathematics.

Organizing Manipulatives for a Classful!

Cindie Heinrich Donahue

Most of the manipulatives I use with my students are stored in plastic bags. The plastic bags with zippers on them work the best because they close easily. I punch a small hole in one of the bottom corners of the bags to deter students from trying to pop them. The hole also helps me squeeze excess air out of the bags for more compact storage. I number and inventory each bag in the set and include a list of the contents with the set.

Students use the same bag of manipulatives each day. The method that works well for me is to assign each student or group of students a specific bag number. I record these assignments and keep them on a clipboard next to the box of manipulatives. To avoid a traffic jam, I release the students by rows or groups to pick up their manipulatives. The students are responsible for inventorying their bags at the beginning of class and telling me if anything is missing. I also try to allow enough time at the end of class for students to put the manipulatives away. I usually assign a student to make sure that the floor is clear of any pieces of manipulatives and that all the bags have been returned.

This same system works well with graphing calculators. I use a gold paint pen to number both the calculators themselves and the covers. The calculators are placed in order on a table, and students are expected to return them to their exact locations at the end of class. I also verify that all calculators have been returned after the monitoring student has done his or her check.

Hands-off Technology Demonstration

The best strategy for demonstrating technology may be a "hands-off" approach. Do not touch the hardware when demonstrating to your students how to use, for example, a spreadsheet or a graphing calculator. Instead, select a student who has limited experience using the technology that is to be demonstrated; have the student follow your directions while using a workstation that is projected to the entire class. You are then free to move about the room while giving directions and monitoring your students' progress. This "hands-off" approach regulates the pace of the presentation, allowing students to keep up with the demonstration and focus on the topic under discussion.

—*Todd Johnson*

Todd Johnson passed away after this tip was accepted for publication.

Notes:

CLASSROOM ASSESSMENT

As a beginning teacher, you have many concerns that you need to address every day. One of your most important concerns is how to determine what your students are learning as a result of their experiences in your classroom. Classroom assessment encompasses much more than simply a test at the end of a unit; it includes every action you take to determine what your students know and understand during every lesson you teach. *Principles and Standards for School Mathematics* (NCTM 2000) states that assessment "should support the learning of important mathematics and furnish useful information to both teachers and students" (p. 11). Assessment should be a component of all mathematics lessons to inform you about your students' learning and guide your instructional decisions.

Uses of Classroom Assessment

Classroom assessment can be a useful tool for both you and your students. Your students can use the information from assessments to set goals and to gauge their progress toward those goals. You can use the information to help make decisions about your teaching. Gathering evidence of students' learning helps you identify those who need additional support or challenges and determine your next instructional steps.

Types of Assessment

Assessments come in a variety of forms, including learning logs, journals, observations, interviews, student self-assessments, performance tasks, projects, portfolios, and more traditional tests. Each assessment technique gives you a different way of looking at your students' understanding; thus, choosing multiple forms of assessment is important in developing a broad picture of what your students know and can do. For example, students can make a presentation to the class about a problem they solved, assess their own use of problem-solving strategies while working on the problem, and select a solution for inclusion in their portfolios.

Planning for Assessment

An essential first step in planning assessments is to identify the mathematics you want students to learn and the evidence you need to gather to determine the extent of their learning. As you plan your lesson, think about what you want your students to learn and how you will know that they have learned it. Assessment should be woven into your lesson as a part of the learning experience. To guide your planning, ask students to write a "K-W-L essay," describing what they *know*, what they *want* to know, and what they *learned*, as you begin and end a unit. Deciding what to assess, what assessment to use, and what you will do with the information gathered from assessment should all be parts of your lesson planning.

Grading Assessments

Grading provides the data you need to use assessments effectively. Different forms of assessment lend themselves to different methods of grading. Sometimes, simply reading and responding to your students' learning logs is sufficient. At other times, you and your students will need to gather more extensive data about their learning. Many assessments can be graded using rubrics. If you choose to use a rubric, consider having your students help you develop the grading criteria before the assessment is given, to clarify your expectations. Be selective in your assessments and how you grade them, however, to ensure that you and your students are not overwhelmed with papers!

As you become more proficient in incorporating assessment into your lessons, gathering and interpreting data from assessment, and using that information to guide your teaching practice, your students will learn more and planning a lesson will become easier and more efficient.

Obviously, classroom assessment is difficult to separate from planning. As a result, you will find assessment ideas throughout this book, not just in this section. In particular, look for ideas in the "Curriculum and Instruction" and "Classroom Management and Organization" sections. As you read this section and think about how you will evaluate your students' understanding, you might keep the following questions in mind:

- What is the important mathematics I want my students to learn, and how will I know that they have learned it?

- What types of assessment do I want to use to gather evidence of student learning, and when is each most appropriate?

- How can my students and I use the data I collect from assessment to improve their learning?

Strategies for Tapping "Hidden" Learners

Mary C. Shafer

As a high school teacher, I try to shape my daily instruction by taking into consideration my students' understanding, insights, and misunderstandings, but I often wonder what those students who rarely engage in classroom conversation know about the mathematics they are learning. I have found the following four methods to be especially effective for opening the lines of communication.

Pair Work

Often, students are more willing to talk when they work in pairs. During pair work, I listen for students' approaches to problems, their understanding of the mathematics, and the mathematical vocabulary they use. I ask students who use unique approaches to explain them in class discussions. In this way, all students learn to see mathematics as a creative process that is within their capabilities.

Journal Writing

Give students opportunities to write in their journals for five to ten minutes once or twice a week. Most students take this assignment seriously because it gives them the opportunity to talk with me directly without other students' becoming aware of their concerns. Students who are shy or popular or whose cultural backgrounds may limit participation in whole-class discussion use the journals as a way to communicate specific needs, difficulties, or successes in understanding concepts. The brief writing tasks provide clues about what students are learning. Over time, I have learned the types of questions that effectively tap into their thinking.

Student Presentations

Some problem solutions are especially good for students to share orally in class, for example, problems set in various contexts that involve application of mathematical concepts. On a given day, each group of three to four students presents a solution to one of several assigned problems. Group presentations provide a forum for acceptable risk taking. Students present the group's solution, not their own, and all members of the group answer questions if the presenter is unsure of a particular aspect. Over time, every student in the class has the opportunity to present a group solution.

Projects

Projects offer opportunities for students to think about mathematics in different ways or to explore applications of mathematics in everyday situations. Every grading period, I ask students to complete one project from a set of eight options that are directly related to the mathematics studied during that grading period. Students may also propose their own ideas for these projects for teacher approval. I display all satisfactory projects in the classroom or school showcases. Students often talk about the projects with other students before and after class. Some students are excited about their projects, ask to talk about them in class, and share their projects with teachers in other disciplines.

Learning Discoveries

Some students in my classes are active talkers, but many are quiet—my "hidden" learners. Through listening to discussions with partners and reading their journals, I continually learn about the content they understand, the types of problems that cause them difficulty, and the misconceptions that they may have developed. I use this information to try different approaches in presenting content and to focus whole-class discussions. In group presentations and projects, students show their peers and me what they are learning and are excited about. In the end, I learn more not only about my students but also about myself and my strengths and weaknesses in teaching them. Using these methods, we all learn and relearn mathematics—and we are enthusiastic about the process.

Student-Developed Rubric:
A Work in Progress

Ranjani Sriram

How can students identify their strengths and weaknesses from a scored assessment and learn from that information? This nagging question led me to create rubrics for scoring certain types of assessments. Specifically, I involved my students in creating a rubric for problem solving. This activity helped them gain an understanding of my expectations for solutions to multistep problems.

Students were assigned to work in groups of three or four. At the start of class, we conducted a brainstorming session to answer the following question: What are the important components of a solution to a multistep problem? We then allocated the ideas that the students offered into five categories that I consider important to assessment: (1) organization, (2) communication, (3) strategy or procedure, (4) accuracy, and (5) completeness. In some classes, I modified this process, listing the five categories first, then having students identify the components of each category.

Each student group was assigned one category. On the basis of the requirements, students used their own words to develop a rubric. That is, for the given category, they had to describe what kind of work would earn ratings of 4, 3, 2, and 1, with 4 as the highest rating. Students displayed their ideas on large pieces of paper. I allotted an entire forty-five–minute period for this activity and conducted it in all five of my classes. At the end of the day, I compiled the information from all classes and made one rubric for all the categories (see fig. 1 [Sriram] on p. 31).

The next day, every student was given a copy of the rubric that they all had created. I told them that I would use this rubric every time I gave problem-solving assessments, and I encouraged them to refer to it when they completed the assessments. Student pairs were then given a few anonymous sample solutions to a word problem that other students had previously completed; the pairs worked to score each of these student samples using the new rubric.

This activity was beneficial for my classes and encouraged student involvement. When students scored the sample problems, I heard such comments as "This is a great way of doing the problem; I never thought of that"; "This step was really not necessary"; "I never thought grading was so much work"; "The work shown makes sense; I get it now"; and "How did they come up with that number?" These comments told me that the students were studying each step carefully and thinking deeply about the process. A follow-up reflection sheet revealed that students valued the rubric-creating activity because the result was written in their language and was easy to understand.

I enlarged the rubric to poster size and had it laminated. Subsequently, when I gave students a problem-solving quiz, they could refer to the rubric during the quiz. They seemed to put a good deal of effort into their work to achieve higher ratings. This activity capitalized on student accountability, responsibility, pride, and involvement—all of which need frequent reinforcement.

Perspectives on Scoring
John E. Hammett III

How can you encourage your mathematics students to value the *process* of solving a problem as much as the *product* of obtaining an appropriate answer to a question? First, avoid answer columns on homework assignments and tests, all-or-nothing grading schemes, and the tendency to label student work as wrong when it is not entirely correct or when it uses a method that differs from yours. Instead, insist on fully detailed mathematical explanations whenever your students solve problems, rewarding every reasonable effort—even those that use a different approach—with positively oriented credit accumulation rather than negatively oriented credit reduction. In other words, use the notation "+2 out of 4 points" instead of "–2 out of 4 points," especially when the solution is incomplete or only partially correct.

Organization

4   All steps are neatly shown. The necessary information is categorized in charts, tables, or lists. All written work is legible, and if necessary, it is in paragraph form.
3   Most work is neatly shown. Charts, tables, or lists are neat, with most of the necessary information organized. Most of the written work is legible.
2   Half the work is missing. Charts, tables, or lists are incomplete. Written work is not too legible.
1   Steps are very unclear. The necessary information has not been organized at all. Written work is illegible.

Communication

4   Explanation of steps is very clear and thorough. All work shows a clear understanding of the problem.
3   Explanation of steps is good but could use more detail. Most work shows an understanding of the problem.
2   Explanation of steps is poor with very little detail. Work shows little understanding of the problem.
1   Very poor explanation with no understanding of how to solve the problem. Work shows no understanding of the problem.

Strategy/Procedure

4   Method and steps used to solve the problem are clearly displayed. Strategy used shows a clear understanding of the problem.
3   Most of the steps used to solve the problem are clearly shown. Strategy used shows a somewhat clear understanding of the problem.
2   Few steps are shown in solving the problem. Strategy does not show an understanding of the problem.
1   Barely any steps shown. Strategy, if any, is random.

Accuracy

4   All calculations are done correctly. All information from the problem is accurately interpreted. Checked to see if answer makes sense.
3   Most calculations are done correctly. Most information from the problem is accurately interpreted. Checked to see if answer makes sense.
2   Half the calculations are done correctly. Information from the problem has not been clearly interpreted. Did not check to see if answer made complete sense.
1   The answer is incorrect. Information from problem is misinterpreted. Answer does not make sense.

Completeness

4   All work is complete. All directions are followed. All questions are answered.
3   Most work is complete. Most directions are followed. Most questions are answered.
2   Half the work is done. Very few directions are followed. Half the questions are answered.
1   Work shows minimal to no effort.

FIGURE 1 (SRIRAM). *Rubric for problem solving*

Tips for a Successful First Year: Testing

Be aware that tests should measure what students know, not what they do not know. Give tests that assess whether students know basic concepts and that allow you to discriminate among levels of understanding.

If you cannot complete your test in a quarter of the time that your students will have to take it, then the students will be unable to complete the test in the time allowed.

—*Agnes M. Rash*

Using Collaborative Testing as an Alternative Form of Assessment

Joan Kwako

One effective way to both gain understanding of students' knowledge and to provide students the opportunity to learn is through collaborative assessment. Collaboration requires students to defend their positions and explain their thinking, which, during a high-stakes situation such as a test, can enhance their learning because of the increased motivation. Collaborative-group tests require students to communicate and participate in groups. However, before you simply assign students randomly into groups and hand them a test, you should make some provisions for the composition of the groups and the type of test administered.

Collaborative Group Size and Heterogeneity

Two factors to consider when assigning groups are size and heterogeneity. I have found that groups of three work best. In a pair, one student may easily dominate the assignment, and in groups of four, some students may get lost in the discussion. Making sure that groups are heterogeneous in terms of gender, status, and ability greatly increases their effectiveness. To ensure heterogeneity of all three factors may seem impossible—and sometimes, it is. Most likely, you will not be able to form perfectly heterogeneous groups, but keeping group composition in mind is important when asking students to complete group tests.

Types of Collaborative Tests

The tests that are administered to groups must be designed differently from those that are given to individual students. Designing questions for a group test is more like creating open-ended homework problems than writing traditional test questions. Collaborative-test problems must require input from all group members; they should not be problems that can be solved by one person working alone. The questions must elicit discussion and encourage students to invest their effort in the solutions. Through these

discussions, students can develop new ideas of their own on the basis of other students' thinking, expose common misconceptions, clarify their thinking, and justify their positions before reaching a group solution.

Another advantage is that this kind of assessment requires you to grade only one-third of the usual number of tests. Competitive students may be unhappy, however, that they are forced to depend on the work of others and may require some guidance in working collaboratively.

The single-solution technique

Another collaborative assessment technique has all group members solve one problem together and write a single solution. Students then individually answer questions about the group solution and solve two similar problems, one that is parallel to the group problem and one that extends it (Kroll, Masingila, and Mau 1996). This approach enables the teacher to calculate both an individual score and a group score. In a variation of this assessment, each student's grade is based on the sum of the group score and the average of the individual scores, resulting in the same grade for each group member. Again, this approach encourages students to commit to helping each of the group members learn the material, because each group member's score depends on the learning of everyone else in the group.

Another variation on this kind of grading includes awarding additional points if all group members score above a certain level on the individual portion of the test. This approach changes the dependence on others for each student's score to a commitment to the learning of all group members, creating a "one for all and all for one" atmosphere. One advantage of this approach is that students have the benefit of learning while taking the group portion of the test but maintain a level of individual accountability. One disadvantage is that fewer concepts can be tested because the three questions for each topic must be parallel in structure. Of course, for the teacher, this approach doubles the number of tests and, thus, the time necessary for testing and grading.

The group take-home examination

Yet another approach to collaborative testing is the group take-home examination. Group members are given seven to ten days to complete the examination and hand in one solution signed by all, and all receive the same grade. In these situations, having group members anonymously grade all other members, including themselves, helps to determine whether everyone contributed equally.

A variation on this technique is the group oral take-home examination (Crannell 1999). In this situation, students are graded entirely on their understanding of the material as they present it; the written work that is handed in is used only to clarify points in their presentations. Students learn from their mistakes because "they get feedback even as they present their results, and since they have debated the results with their teammates, they care about the answer" (Crannell 1999, p. 144). The longer time allowed for this kind of assessment enables high-level conceptual problems to be included on the test, and students can learn a great deal when researching the answers to such problems. Teachers may have difficulty, however, determining whether all group members contributed equally and what each group member knows individually.

Benefits and Drawbacks of Collaborative Testing

When administering group tests, keep in mind that students have probably not experienced similar assessments in the past. Some will revel in the idea; others will find it frustrating. Time spent on discussing effective group interactions may be helpful before implementing group tests.

Collaborative tests have many benefits: they are more realistic in terms of what students will face in the world of work in the future; they reduce the anxiety surrounding testing; they mimic more closely the actions of mathematicians; they increase students' potential to succeed; and most important, they afford students the opportunity to learn.

Conclusion

This list of ideas for group testing is short. However, it may be enough to encourage you to consider assessment strategies other than the traditional lineup of homework, quizzes, and tests and to think of assessment as an opportunity for students to learn cooperatively.

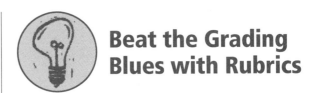

Beat the Grading Blues with Rubrics

Gina Garza-Kling

Writing a rubric before grading a test takes a few minutes initially but saves time and energy in the long run because it makes the grading process much more efficient. As you create the response key, you can also create a rubric for each problem. This rubric indicates the specific components that are needed in each solution for points to be awarded. As you write the rubric, try to predict and account for possible student errors. The following is an example of a rubric for a test item that assesses application of the distance formula:

Solution

$$D = \sqrt{(x_2 - x_1)^2 + (y_2 - y_1)^2}$$
$$= \sqrt{(0-5)^2 + (12-0)^2}$$
$$= \sqrt{25 + 144}$$
$$= \sqrt{169}$$
$$= 13$$

Rubric

Score	Explanation
0	Work is unfocused or shows no effort.
1	Student wrote down distance formula correctly or demonstrated another appropriate strategy but did not find a solution.
2	Student set up solution correctly but made a small error in execution, such as— • did not take square root, • confused x- and y-coordinates, or • took square root of each term before adding.
3	Student found the correct solution.

Tests are not designed to allow students to accumulate a certain number of points but, rather, to gauge their understanding and achievement. Rubrics facilitate this assessment because points are never assigned arbitrarily. Each point awarded is a direct result of a correct step in the solution process.

Rubrics offer students clear feedback and allow teachers to justify how points are awarded for a particular assessment. Furthermore, they facilitate consistent grading, especially with late assignments or makeup work. Rubrics are effective tools for assessment, and I encourage you to use them as part of your regular teaching practice.

Using Notes during Tests

Todd Johnson

Before the first test in a mathematics class, students sometimes ask, "Can we use notes on the test?" In my class, students are often allowed to use notes when taking tests, but I limit the notes a student may use to one page. Additionally, students' notes must be submitted at the beginning of class the day before the test.

Allowing students to use notes during tests has several benefits, including the following:

- Students must review and synthesize their class notes to make a useful page of test notes.

- Because they must submit their notes the day before the test, students spend at least two nights studying.

- While making their pages of test notes, students come up with good questions to ask in class the day before the test.

- After collecting students' notes, the teacher can pinpoint concepts that students think are important to know for the test, identify students who might have difficulty learning particular concepts, and detect errors in students' thinking.

- Finally, students may become aware that tests do not always emphasize the recall of memorized information but often emphasize the application of that information.

Todd Johnson passed away after the writing of this item was completed. The editors have chosen to leave the text in the present tense, as it was prepared.

Notes:

4 SECTION

CLASSROOM MANAGEMENT AND ORGANIZATION

Experienced teachers tend to use a variety of methods to manage and organize their classrooms. In contrast, beginning teachers may wander the halls during the days before the start of school, peering into the classrooms of experienced teachers in search of ideas about how to arrange the room for that first day, how to set expectations that keep students on task, and how to keep track of students' work when they do stay on task! As a new teacher, the resources you find to address these concerns will influence your own strategies for management and organization and help you create a pleasant and productive learning environment. During your beginning years of teaching, among your first priorities should be the need to organize your classroom and manage the instructional environment in ways that support, rather than impede, students' learning of mathematics. The following paragraphs highlight some important aspects of classroom management and organization.

Set Clear Expectations

Of course, your students are required to abide by your institution's rules and regulations, but you should also establish expectations regarding how your students should treat one another in the classroom and how they should accomplish their work. Do not hesitate to inform your students of these expectations and the consequences of not living up to them. Be fair and consistent in holding students to these expectations.

Know One Another

Whether you are with your students for the entire school day or for only a single class period, arrange opportunities to converse with them. In the same manner that you are different from every other teacher, each student is also unique. One of the joys of teaching is getting to know each student as an individual. You should also provide opportunities for students to interact with one another. Building a sense of community is one important way to create an effective instructional environment in which students can learn mathematics.

Organize People, Space, and Materials

Try a variety of arrangements for individual and group work to meet students' differing needs and keep them engaged in learning. As you get to know your students, you will be able to select appropriate arrangements for different tasks. Keep in mind, however, that students also need chances to try new methods. For instance, a student who seems to work best alone might be asked to work with a partner on a more complex task to help the "loner" become more comfortable working in a group.

You may also try different strategies to organize your space and materials. Experienced teachers have many wonderful ideas for arranging classrooms, making efficient use of closets, or setting up filing systems. Be on the lookout for new ideas, but always consider them in light of your style and your students' needs. Remember that the goal is for students to learn mathematics; your methods for organizing people, space, and materials should always contribute to—not detract from—your students' learning opportunities.

Manage Time

You will soon learn that in teaching, you never have enough time! As you gain experience, you will develop ways to save more time for instruction. Learn to build natural "breaking points" into lessons that are difficult to teach as a whole in the time allowed. As you become more familiar with the required record keeping, look for ways to reduce time spent on that task, perhaps involving students or parent volunteers. Every few weeks, evaluate one hour of your instructional time to see whether you could make better use of the time by changing some small aspect of classroom management or organization.

Assess Strategies for Organization

Not all management tools will work for all teachers. As you read this section and experiment with different strategies for classroom management and organization, you might evaluate each strategy by asking the following questions:

- How does this management or organizational idea contribute to a classroom environment that supports students' learning of mathematics?

- How does this idea help me better organize my students, space, or materials so that I can use instructional time more efficiently?

- How can I involve students in developing ideas for classroom management and organization to build their sense of ownership in the instructional environment?

Questioning My Frustration to Uncover My Expectations

Clint Kaufmann

Like many teachers, I have been frustrated by students' tardiness, rudeness, shoddy work, poor organization, and lackluster efforts. In a process that I call *questioning frustration,* I use four questions to prompt myself to uncover, articulate, and address my expectations that students are failing to meet. The four questions are these:

1. What unmet expectation underlies this frustration?
2. How can I clearly communicate the expectation?
3. How can I hold students accountable if they fail to meet the expectation?
4. How can I help students meet the expectation?

The following paragraphs describe how I might use these prompts to question my frustration with mildly disruptive behavior in the classroom.

Identifying Unmet Expectations

Students' conduct is an ongoing concern for all teachers. I have used countless moments of class time to interrupt off-task chats, ask for attention, or position myself near snickering students. I find that a series of mild, perhaps seemingly harmless, disruptions can steer a class's focus away from the lesson. I finally asked myself, "What unmet expectation underlies my frustration with the effects of these minor disruptions?" Although I wished that students would refrain from all off-task behavior, I accepted that some is inevitable. I articulated the expectation that no student would be a consistent source of disruption, even if the disruptive behavior was mild.

Communicating Expectations

I next asked, "How can I clearly communicate this expectation?" Never having focused on communicating expectations, I had relied on a first-day-of-school admonition on the importance of good conduct and scattered scoldings and detentions. Experience suggested that I should use consistent and ongoing communication; thus, I found opportunities to remind students of my conduct expectation. For example, when Lacy came to the front of the classroom to present a problem, I reminded the class, "Remember that during a whole-class discussion, one person speaks at a time. Lacy will lead this discussion." Simple reminders, coupled with a consistently implemented system of accountability, have proved to be effective communication tools.

Holding Students Accountable for Disruptive Behavior

My next question was "How can I hold students accountable for behaving disruptively?" I devised a simple system of warnings and interventions. During a class period, I issue and record a warning for a student's first offense. Subsequent disruptions are recorded and result in classroom-level interventions. If these measures prove unsuccessful, I resort to speaking with a parent and reporting the student to the dean.

Helping Students Meet Expectations

Consistent communication and accountability sufficiently encourage most students to conduct themselves appropriately; however, some students require special attention. Thus, I asked myself the last of my four questions: "How can I help students meet my conduct expectation?" One student, David, was chronically disruptive. Sometimes, he seemed unaware of the inappropriateness of his behavior. I began to speak privately with him about his conduct, regularly evaluating his behavior and giving him specific suggestions for improvement. David responded well to the individual attention, which proved to be an effective communication tool in helping him meet my conduct expectation.

I use similar questions to explore my frustration with many other issues, such as tardiness, seemingly unmotivated students, or lack of perseverance in problem solving. Questioning my frustration with disruptive behavior prompts me to uncover my conduct expectation, to articulate it, and to take action that is consistent with it. I find that classroom management is an ongoing process of revisiting my four questions and reconsidering my teaching methods.

Dealing with Disruptive Students

David Thomas

Dealing with disruptive behavior need not be an emotionally exhausting or demoralizing experience. My response to it is based on three simple principles. First, remain calm and professional in the face of provocation. Second, be fair and accurate in recording the objective details of any offense. Third, frame discussions with students, colleagues, and parents in terms of those records. To implement these principles, keep a spiral-bound notebook with you at all times. In this notebook, carefully record exceptional in-class behavior, both good and bad, and achievements as they occur. For instance, if a student disrupts class or otherwise engages in unacceptable behavior, pause, take out the notebook, and record the disruption as follows:

1. Write a brief description of the student's behavior, avoiding sweeping characterizations, prejudicial comments, and unprofessional language. Simply state what happened, not how you felt about it.
2. Read your description to the offending student and any other students involved in the incident as "victims" or "witnesses." Ask for factual corrections or clarifications.
3. Remind the disruptive student that you are prepared to share your notes with his or her parents and the school administration if necessary.

4. Make an appointment to see the offending student outside of class. This policy gives you adequate time to think calmly about the offense; it also gives the student time to worry about the potential consequences.

A similar record can be made when a student demonstrates exceptional insight, generosity, or some other exemplary trait. Each entry should be dated to enable individual events to be seen in sequence and in context. Notes from follow-up meetings with students, counselors, and parents can also be kept in the same notebook.

Although creating entries of this sort can take a few minutes in class, the impact on general classroom behavior is well worth the time spent. On occasions when you need to "rein in" a particular student, eye contact, followed by a tap on the notebook, might often be enough to achieve the desired effect, thus avoiding confrontation or other students' awareness of your actions. My advice to beginning teachers is the following: Find some version of this approach that works for you, and implement it as a matter of routine. Then relax, and allow the routine to take the place of your frustration or anger. Instituting this system will build your reputation for high standards, professionalism, and fair treatment.

Something I Never Learned in Methods Class: Practice Selective Hearing

Do not comment on everything students say in your classroom. Sometimes, the wise teacher practices selective hearing. Do create a classroom atmosphere that encourages students to treat one another with respect.

—*Margaret R. Meyer*

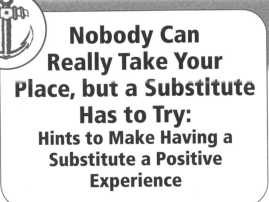

Nobody Can Really Take Your Place, but a Substitute Has to Try:
Hints to Make Having a Substitute a Positive Experience

Nancy Powell
Cathy Denbesten

Not knowing when you might need a substitute can be stressful; however, being organized can lessen the stress and enable you to avoid last-minute preparations. One helpful organizational technique is to create a substitute notebook that can remain in your classroom. Label the notebook clearly, and leave it in a prominent place or make sure that a colleague knows where to find it in the event you are absent. Organize and mark sections to ensure that a substitute can understand and refer to the notebook easily.

Information for a Substitute Binder

Suggestions for information to include in the substitute binder are listed below.

- A welcome note that thanks the substitute for coming and provides helpful information, such as the handiest place to hang a coat or safely stash a purse, the names and room numbers of teachers in nearby classrooms who are able to answer general or mathematics-related questions, and instructions on where to find needed lesson-plan books

- Classroom rules and regulations, including suggested discipline procedures and locations of detention or discipline forms and hall passes; clear plastic sheet protectors to house copies of these forms in the binder

- A procedure for getting help or contacting the office

- General procedures for fire drills, tornado drills, injuries, and so on

- Forms that need to be filled out every day, and instructions on where to find them

- A chronological list of class periods, including lunch, and times or days that are scheduled for extra duties

- Accurate seating charts with the name that each student commonly uses and attendance sheets that can be carried out of the classroom in an evacuation. Many grade-book software programs include options for printing seating charts with students' pictures, which can be helpful for substitutes.

- Notes for each class that include—
  - ✓ the names of helpful, trustworthy students;
  - ✓ the names of students who have special medical needs or may need emergency care;
  - ✓ the names of non-English-speaking students or students who are enrolled in English as a second language; and
  - ✓ any other important information of which a substitute should be aware

- Clear, understandable lesson plans with instructions about where to find necessary handouts, materials, and supplies for the lesson; notes or keys for worksheets, tests, or quizzes; and an optional activity for each class in the event that students finish their assigned work

- Special activities that can be used any time of the year in an emergency

- A place to leave notes regarding behavior, absences, accomplishments, and questions, by class

Reminders for Students

Spend a few minutes talking to your classes about your expectations for them when you are absent. Remind students that the reason they are in class is to learn and that they need to use every opportunity to do so whether or not you are physically present. When you return, address any issues documented by the substitute. Do not ignore even minor misbehavior unless you want to hear about more problems the next time you are absent.

A "MUST-DO" LIST

A "MUST-DO" ORGANIZATION LIST FOR BEGINING MATHEMATICS TEACHERS

Jane M. Till-Schröder

Regardless of setting, these general planning guidelines are helpful for all mathematics teachers:

1. Request copies of the student and teacher handbooks immediately after signing your contract. Begin to formulate your own classroom rules using the general school parameters listed in the handbooks.

2. Read and highlight the student handbook for important policies that you and your students will follow on a daily basis.

3. Consider using Power Point to present important classroom information. Print out slides, and use them around the classroom as posters. Alternatively, give a slide show on the first day of classes. Slides may include—

   • classroom rules for behavior,

   • inspirational words,

   • bell schedules, and

   • classroom policies on grading and attendance.

4. Ask what supplies the school provides. These should include pencils, erasers, rulers, lined paper, graph paper, construction paper, transparency films for the classroom and the photocopier, transparency markers, thick permanent markers, and red pens.

5. Create your own storage system, including shelves to organize paperwork for different classes; label the shelves clearly so that students can tell them apart.

6. Have seating charts prepared for the first day of school to send a strong message to any student who is intent on disrupting your class. Make changes throughout the semester as necessary.

7. In the first day of school, hand a blank index card to each student and request any information you think you may need, such as—

   • full name,

   • emergency contact names and telephone numbers,

   • extracurricular activities, and

   • special classroom accommodations necessary to succeed.

8. Post a bell schedule in the room, perhaps near the clock. Having this schedule handy will help you as much as the students.

9. Students are only as organized as their teacher. Take the initiative, and enforce some rules for organization:
   - Require all notes and assignments to be kept in one place.
   - Have students head every paper with their full names, the name of the course, the date, and the assignment.

10. Make sure students record each assignment and corresponding score. This record will help both students and their parents track their progress and, perhaps, stop asking you to do it for them! Use this procedure for each class:

    - Distribute an assignment sheet to be affixed to the inside cover of students' notebooks.
    - Make a folder for each class, and affix the assignment sheet inside the cover to allow students who have been absent to find assignments easily.

11. Keep a large three-ring binder for each subject you teach, complete with the curriculum designed for the class placed in the front. Maintain this binder by following these practices:

    - As you complete each unit, place important masters, keys, handouts, and assessments in the binder.
    - Color-code and flag items that emphasize a particular standard.
    - Keep copies of students' work to demonstrate that standards were met.

Seating-Chart Notebook

I make a notebook containing seating charts for each of my classes in clear plastic sheet protectors. Using a fine-tip overhead-projector pen, I write directly on the sheet protectors to record attendance, tardies, and homework grades. Later in the day, I quickly transfer this information into my grade book. This system saves valuable time while students are in class and helps to keep my grade book neater.

—*Cindie Heinrich Donahue*

Topic Files as an Organizational Tool for the Classroom
Susie Tummers

As it is in almost any career, organization is essential to success in teaching. The organizational tool that has proved to be most beneficial during my career is my system of *topic files*. As a beginning teacher, I collected the work that I did for a particular class and placed all of it in a three-ring binder. Difficulty arose in subsequent years when I attempted to locate a particular lesson or activity. The binder was quite full, and locating specific items became a problem; hence, the topic-file strategy was born.

For each course I teach, I make a list of topics. I place these topics in file folders to start my hanging-file system. Each folder contains activities, lessons, worksheets, and so on, that pertain to that topic. When the time comes to teach a certain topic, I can easily locate the folder that contains a collection of all the information I have on that subject and begin to plan my lesson.

I have found three significant benefits to maintaining topic files. First, the files are an effective organizational tool. All topics are organized, and each file is within quick reach. If an activity or lesson focuses on more than one topic, I can easily make a few photocopies and place the duplicate information in as many topic files as is appropriate. Second, topic files provide a place for me to keep the lessons that colleagues share with me and, in turn, enable me to share ideas with colleagues. I am delighted when teachers come to my classroom asking whether I have a file on a particular topic. Third, the files are a wonderful way to organize the material I receive at the professional development conferences that I attend. When I return from a conference, I simply place photocopies of the lessons and notes in the appropriate files.

Topic files offer an organizational strategy that can work for beginning teachers at all grade levels and in all disciplines. This flexible system can easily be tailored to suit your specific needs, modified to accommodate textbook changes, or moved if you transfer to a new school. This simple idea may seem trivial, but it is one that I wish I had learned earlier in my own career.

Organizing Tests and Important Papers

Susan Kyle Arn

Organization is important to teachers, and students can learn to appreciate its benefits, as well. One system I use is to designate a different color of paper for each type of printed material that I distribute in class. For example, all practice exercises might be on pink paper, and I would not use that color for anything else. In my classroom, tests are always on yellow paper, vocabulary lists are on blue, and review pages are on green. Students learn this system quickly, and it helps them organize their notebooks and portfolios. When students are reviewing for quarter or semester examinations, colored-coded papers help them organize information and allow them to study more efficiently. As a teacher, I have also become more organized by using this system when preparing and filing classroom materials.

Something I Never Learned in Methods Class: Preventing "Invisible" Students

Do not let students become invisible in your classroom. Greet them by name when they enter the classroom. Comment on their accomplishments in sports and clubs. Consider how you might use information about students' interests as bases for investigations in your mathematics class, thereby piquing students' interest and involvement in the tasks.

—*Margaret R. Meyer*

Notes:

5 SECTION

EQUITY

As a beginning teacher, you will need to think about how to achieve equity in your mathematics classroom. An important resource to consult in your efforts is the Equity Principle in *Principles and Standards for School Mathematics* (NCTM 2000). This principle offers a broad outline for implementing practices that serve all students. This section complements that discussion by introducing several important ideas to consider for the students who may enter your classroom from diverse backgrounds. In particular, be aware of the issues outlined in the following paragraphs.

Evaluate Your Own Beliefs and Biases

Evaluating your own beliefs about, and biases toward, school mathematics as a discipline and about your students' learning of school mathematics is essential. To begin your reflection, you might ask yourself the following questions and try to answer candidly:

- How do I learn mathematics?
- What are some ways in which my students learn mathematics most effectively?
- Do I believe that only certain students in my classroom can learn mathematics? If so, why do I hold those beliefs?
- What expectations do I hold for my students?
- Do my beliefs and biases limit my students' opportunities to learn mathematics?
- How might I change my beliefs and biases to ensure that I promote opportunities for my students to learn mathematics?

Most likely, your responses to these types of questions will dictate your daily teaching practices and habits. As you become more aware of equity issues and more committed to making necessary accommodations to "promote access and attainment for all students" (NCTM 2000, p. 12), your own beliefs may change; in turn, you will influence your students' beliefs through the expectations you convey to them about their learning of mathematics.

Consider the Commitment

Beginning and experienced teachers alike should realize that maintaining educational equity requires a substantial commitment. You may be called on to invest considerable time and energy in activities to ensure equitable conditions in your classroom and school. Whether alone or with colleagues, you should brainstorm strategies to ensure fairness in your teaching and implementation of school policies and curricula. You may have to collaborate with colleagues to develop better understandings of the "strengths and needs of students who come from diverse linguistic and cultural backgrounds, who have specific disabilities, or who possess a special talent and interest in mathematics" (NCTM 2000, p. 14). Certainly, you should explore the literature about equity issues to continue your professional growth in this area and increase your sense of dedication to your students' mathematical achievement.

Teach Students, Then the Subject

Initially, this perspective may seem awkward, but keep in mind that regardless of the subject or the students' backgrounds, you are first teaching *individuals.* Establishing a good rapport with your students and setting high academic expectations for them are important. Further, you should vary the ways in which you conduct mathematics instruction to ensure that students relate to your teaching and perform to your levels of expectation.

Learn More about Equity Issues

Examine the readings in this section to learn more about teaching mathematics to females, students who have special needs, and culturally diverse students, including English-language learners. These readings may shed light on your understanding of the strengths and needs of students who look, speak, or behave differently than you did as a student or than you do now as an adult.

Research Findings Involving English-Language Learners and Implications for Mathematics Teachers

Sylvia Celedón-Pattichis

To help you build support for English-language learners in your classroom, the following paragraphs describe some terminology and research findings that address language-acquisition issues affecting mathematics teaching and learning.

Learning Language through Silence

English-language learners need a *silent period* (Baker 2001), that is, time to acquire the new language without necessarily producing it. This period often lasts two to five months and can be as long as a year. This silence should not be interpreted as unwillingness to participate in mathematics classroom activities. Teachers might use cooperative learning or pairing of students to ensure that English-language learners are exposed to the new language in nonthreatening ways.

Acquiring Social and Academic Language

English-language learners usually acquire basic interpersonal communication skills, or the *social language,* on the playground, through peer conversations, and in other informal settings during their first two years in a new culture. However, they need five to seven years or more to use the academic language required in educational content areas. The ability to use the language needed to perform in an educational context is referred to as *cognitive academic language proficiency* (Cummins, as cited in Baker [2001]).

Basic interpersonal communication skills are usually learned in *context-embedded* situations. For example, the act of talking face-to-face and using nonverbal gestures with students gives them instant feedback and clues to support spoken language. In contrast, cognitive academic language proficiency tends to be *context reduced,* meaning that no clues are available to support comprehension. Mathematics is often taught abstractly, but for English-

language learners, the subject must be put into context with, for example, diagrams or the students' own definitions, especially when students are being introduced to new vocabulary and word problems.

Developing the Mathematics Register

The *mathematics register* (Halliday 1978), or the specific language used in mathematics, is often problematic for English-language learners. Contrary to popular belief, mathematics is not a universal language. The mathematics register contains many words that have different meanings from what students initially expect. Educators should distinguish between the meanings of words that overlap in the everyday use of English and in mathematics. Teachers can use many strategies to develop the mathematics register in their students, including reinterpreting words in the everyday language, such as *point, reduce, carry, set, power,* and *root.*

Making Appropriate Placements

The Third International Mathematics and Science Study indicates that the U.S. eighth-grade mathematics curriculum is at a seventh-grade level in comparison with that of other countries (United States Department of Education 1997). Thus, care should be taken in placing English-language learners in mathematics classes to avoid repetition of content. Follow these procedures when determining placement of students from other countries:

- Use test results as supplementary information only.

- Ensure that students have a translator who can help them understand examination instructions and that the translator explains the purpose of the test results.

- If a textbook is available, compare and contrast the curriculum used in the student's previous country with that of the United States.

- Negotiate possible placements by talking to teachers, parents, the student, and counselors. If the student needs to take a mathematics course that is offered at a higher grade level, then the school district should make that option available.

- Ask for previous school contact information from the student or the family to learn what mathematical skills the student demonstrated in his or her previous school.

Sharing Learners' Cultures in the Classroom

To establish a positive learning environment, mathematics educators should consider the linguistic and cultural experiences that English-language learners bring to the classroom. For example, if a student uses a different algorithm for division, demonstrate it to the class to create a learning moment for everyone. Finally, research students' backgrounds and seek the help of bilingual teachers or specialists in English as a second language to help your students adjust to their new culture.

Tips for Teaching Culturally Diverse Students

Joan Cohen Jones

As a beginning mathematics teacher, I taught in a culturally and ethnically diverse district in the southeastern United States. My students were recent immigrants from Africa, Asia, and Mexico. Our soccer team had representatives from seventeen countries, and our PTA newsletter was printed in nine languages. During my first year, I remember becoming frustrated with a Cambodian student who would not look at me when I spoke to him. Only later did I learn that in his culture, this behavior was a sign of respect rather than disrespect. This experience helped me realize that my lack of knowledge about students' cultural backgrounds hampered my ability to communicate with them effectively.

While I learned more about my students' cultures, I also developed effective strategies for teaching mathematics to diverse students. The following tips are drawn from my experiences as a teacher, student-teaching supervisor, and teacher educator. These strategies can work for all students, but they are specifically designed to create positive experiences for culturally diverse students. They are appropriate for all grade levels and can easily be adapted to other disciplines.

Check for existing knowledge

When planning for instruction, decide what concepts students need to know to learn the new material. Include checks for existing knowledge at the beginning of your lessons. If necessary, restructure your lessons to develop the requisite knowledge.

Listen to what students say

Listen to students' comments, questions, and responses. Only by listening carefully can you learn what your students know, what they misunderstand, what is important for them to learn, and what are the best ways for them to learn.

Question students to reinforce learning and build students' confidence

Ask questions to reinforce students' learning, for example, "How do you know?" "Who knows how to find the answer?" "Will that approach always work?" "Have you seen other problems like this one before?" "Can you find a pattern?" Such questions encourage students to give explanations, search for connections, and rely on themselves and their peers, building self-reliance, cooperation, respect, and confidence.

Increase wait time during classroom discourse

Increasing your wait time during classroom discourse enhances your listening and questioning skills and improves communication. When listening to students' questions, for example, wait until they are finished speaking instead of cutting in after you think you know what is being asked. Pause for several seconds before trying to answer the question yourself or asking someone else to answer it. Then repeat the question to make sure that you understand what is being asked. When a teacher really listens, students are encouraged to ask the questions they might otherwise keep to themselves. Being given extra time to answer can also be helpful to female students and students whose first language is not English.

Respect students' abilities and competence

Demonstrate respect for your students' abilities and competence by giving them high-level intellectual tasks that require complex processing and critical thinking.

Doing so conveys your confidence that they can master the material.

Become familiar with and respect students' cultures

Find out as much as possible about each culture represented in your class. Parents and other family members are wonderful resources to help you learn about your students' backgrounds. If possible, spend some time in the neighborhood in which your school is located. Shop at the local grocery store, participate in neighborhood festivals and celebrations, eat at local restaurants, and become familiar with community activities. This practice can enhance your cultural understanding.

Be reflective

Become a reflective practitioner. That is, monitor, review, and revise your practices, instructional choices, and methodology consistently to ensure that you are being fair and open-minded, providing high-level tasks for your students, and connecting your students' cultural backgrounds with new concepts. An important step in reflection is to think about your own cultural heritage and understand your own biases. Reflection lets you review your own actions in light of what you know about yourself, including your strengths, weaknesses, biases, and prejudices. Some teachers find that keeping a journal, making records of class discussions, or videotaping their classroom instruction is helpful in this process.

Offer students choices

Offer your students instructional choices. Student choice is especially important for culturally diverse students, who may have learning styles that differ from those of their peers in the dominant culture. When developing classroom activities, offer choices in assignments and types of assessments; give students the opportunity to work independently, in pairs, or in small groups; and allow students to respond in oral or written form, individually, in teams, or as a class.

Enjoy the challenge

Teaching mathematics to diverse students can be challenging but extremely rewarding—both personally and professionally. I hope the ideas discussed here are helpful as you begin your career in education.

Perspectives on Meeting the Needs of Special Learners in the High School Mathematics Class

Julie A. Sliva

One of the most important lessons I learned in my first year of teaching high school mathematics was how to teach a wide range of students, including those with special needs. One of my most memorable students was Amanda, a ninth grader in my prealgebra class. Amanda was fidgety in the classroom and never seemed to pay attention. Often, she did not complete homework assignments, and her performance on assessments deteriorated as the year progressed. Although I understood that her lack of attention in class could inhibit her progress, she was able to answer correctly almost any question I asked her out loud; thus, I was puzzled about why she was not successful on tests. She also appeared to understand the material when I worked with her individually in class and after school.

Identifying Requirements of Individual Special Needs Learners

Amanda had an individualized education plan to which I had access through her special education teacher. From this teacher, previous mathematics teachers, and her parents, I learned valuable information that gave me a better understanding of Amanda. I found out, for example, that Amanda had a reason for fidgeting in class; she was diagnosed with attention deficit disorder (ADD). Amanda was responsible for taking her own Ritalin, a medication often prescribed for individuals with ADD, but at times, she forgot to do so; by the time she reached mathematics class, she had difficulty paying attention, and she knew it. Together, her parents, Amanda, her special education teacher, and I crafted a plan to help Amanda succeed in class. To help alleviate the attention problem, we suggested that Amanda set the alarm on her watch to remind her to take her medication. Because Amanda still had some difficulty concentrating, we worked out a few signals that would cue her to pay attention in class. These techniques ranged from calling her name to answer a question to tapping a finger on her desk as I walked by.

I also discovered that Amanda was more inclined toward auditory learning than visual learning; for that reason, she found that questions were easier to answer if they were asked orally rather than written on a test paper. Further, I learned that the format of my tests tended to confuse Amanda because the questions were too close together on the page. To address this problem, I left more white space around the questions when I prepared Amanda's tests. To offer further support, her special education teacher read these questions aloud to her in the resource room. With these strategies, Amanda did increasingly well as the year progressed and learned a great deal of mathematics.

As a new teacher, I was unaware of the many special needs that learners could have and still be in the same pre-algebra class! I was also unaware of the many modifications that could be made for these students. Finally, in attempting to meet the needs of other special needs students that year, I discovered that many of the same strategies were effective for all learners.

Interferences with Special Needs Students' Learning

The following are some of the issues that may interfere with a special needs student's ability to learn mathematics:

- Understanding such concepts as *first* and *greater than*
- Remembering information
- Mentally shifting from one task to the next
- Developing essential perceptual skills, such as the ability to see spatial and size relationships and understand sequencing
- Developing fluency with mathematics facts
- Maintaining positive attitudes toward learning mathematics
- Selecting appropriate strategies to solve problems
- Reasoning

Support Strategies for Special Needs Learners

Many strategies that support special education students have also been found to be effective for all students. Such strategies may include the following:

- Preteaching vocabulary
- Using concrete manipulatives to teach abstract concepts
- Introducing multiple representations
- Using real-world applications
- Modeling problem solving
- Promoting a positive attitude toward learning mathematics
- Assisting students in their development of strategies
- Increasing students' exposure to material

Bringing special needs students into the regular classroom expands the already wide range of abilities and experiences of the students as a group and may make the task of meeting all learners' needs seem daunting, even to an experienced teacher. An important factor in meeting this educational challenge is collaboration. New teachers may not always know a variety of strategies to help students. Working with experienced mathematics teachers and other school resources can help you learn these valuable techniques.

Mathematics Instruction That Works for Girls

Abbe H. Herzig
Rebecca Ambrose
Olof Steinthorsdottir

Mathematics instruction has traditionally catered to a small segment of the population. We encourage you to consider some of the following suggestions gleaned from educational research for making your mathematics instruction accessible to all students, especially girls.

Vary instructional strategies

Discourse has become an important element in mathematics classes, but it does not always have to be conducted in a whole-class setting. Students who are less assertive or less confident about speaking publicly—as many girls are—are less likely to participate actively in whole-class discussions. Working cooperatively with their peers in small groups gives students opportunities to engage actively in mathematics in a less threatening environment.

Too often, mathematics classes become the site of competition, with students being encouraged to be the fastest and the brightest. Some students, including many females, find this kind of competition distasteful and resist participating in it. Group work can create a supportive environment in which the emphasis is on learning together instead of surpassing other students. Many girls prefer this environment.

Although individual seatwork or whole-class discussions might work best for certain types of lessons, group work is often an effective way to engage all students in performing high-quality mathematics tasks. Different students flourish in different environments, and by varying the types of work you do in class, you give more students opportunities to do their best.

Focus on understanding and problem solving

When mathematics is taught as an abstract set of rules and recipes for solving various categories of problems, students learn to solve those specific problems but may not be able to use that knowledge in other contexts. Some research suggests that even though all students, boys and girls, prefer to understand the mathematics they are studying, girls will distance themselves from mathematics when they do not understand it, whereas boys are less bothered by a lack of understanding. When students learn mathematics with understanding, they are able to use that knowledge as a foundation for further learning.

Instead of focusing on correct answers, make problem-solving strategies the primary emphasis of your instruction. By examining your students' strategies, you will start to learn what they understand and can plan future instruction accordingly. Encourage your students to explain their reasoning and to actively listen to, question, and learn from, one another. They will discover that mathematics makes sense, and more students will maintain their interest in the subject.

Make mathematics meaningful

Students who do not see the use for mathematics are less likely to stay interested in it. Girls seem to be particularly sensitive to issues of relevance in mathematics. Problems that are set in meaningful contexts can be excellent motivation for students who need to see the relevance of what they do. The contexts chosen should be interesting and relevant to all students in your class, both girls and boys. Too often, mathematics problems focus on topics that interest boys, without a balance of problems that appeal to girls. As you get to know your students, you can choose problem contexts that are most meaningful to them; doing so can also be a great way to engage students of diverse ethnic backgrounds. You can also ask students to write problems for others in the class to solve. This exercise can be a helpful way to involve students, learn how they think about mathematics, and develop meaningful problem contexts.

Use a deliberate strategy for calling on students

In whole-class discussions, boys tend to raise their hands faster than girls. If you call on the first person who responds to a question, you leave out those students who require more time to think about the question and formulate responses. Research shows that girls still tend to be less assertive and may need time to develop confidence before raising their hands. Experiment with different strategies for getting more students involved in class discussions. Always give students plenty of time to think before calling on anyone. You might try silently counting to ten before choosing a student to respond to a question. You might also call out names for responses instead of choosing students who have raised their hands, to ensure that everyone has equal opportunities to participate.

Examine the types of feedback you give students

Some research shows that teachers interact with students in different ways—most likely, without realizing it. In responding to students' work, teachers sometimes ask boys more sophisticated and challenging questions than they ask girls. Because most teachers are probably unaware of this behavior, we should all continually reflect on how we talk to our students. Be sure to reward all students' progress equally and ask them all questions that challenge them to think more deeply about mathematics.

Maintain high expectations for all students

Research shows that when teachers have different expectations for different students, their interactions with students reflect those expectations. If a teacher does not believe that a student has high potential—because of the student's race, gender, disability, or ethnicity, for example—then the teacher may be satisfied with a lower level of performance from that individual than from a student who the teacher thinks is more capable. Further, students are likely to live up, or down, to the teacher's expectations. In your classroom, maintain high expectations for all students because all are capable of learning mathematics with understanding.

Making Group Work Effective in the Mathematics Classroom

Abbe H. Herzig
David T. S. Kung

Research shows that when a girl is outnumbered by boys in a group, the boys may exclude her or she may be relegated to lower-level tasks. She may feel intimidated and withdraw from the work. If you encounter this situation, address it with the students and help them learn to interact more equitably. You can also rearrange the groups to include at least two girls, or no girls, in each group. Boys who are in the minority in a group are less likely to have this problem. Similar problems can arise with students of different ethnic or racial backgrounds. Although research has found that working in diverse groups helps foster students' understanding of others' cultures and backgrounds, teachers should teach students to work together productively and should monitor the work of groups closely to ensure that each student feels comfortable participating.

Some teachers prefer to assign students to mixed-ability groups, whereas others separate students of different ability levels. Here, the research is fairly clear: both the stronger and the weaker students benefit when they work together; some research even shows that the stronger students benefit more because they enhance their own understanding as they explain concepts to others. Struggling students also learn from observing the effective problem-solving behaviors modeled by stronger students.

Notes:

6 SECTION

SCHOOL AND COMMUNITY

Although you will undoubtedly find yourself very busy in your first year of teaching, you will need to find time to reach out to parents and the surrounding school community. In addition to learning more about your students, you will discover that establishing relationships with parents and the community will yield the resources and support required to be successful. When teachers, parents, and the community act together, students benefit in numerous ways. This cooperation often leads to increased rates of attendance, improved academic achievement and graduation rates, and generally better attitudes about school.

Parents are your students' first teachers and your greatest resource. Parents can provide you with valuable information about their children's interests, attitudes, environment, habits, and aptitudes. Parents can be your staunch allies and partners, encouraging their children to persevere and achieve in mathematics. To tap this important resource, often, you only have to reach out and invite parents into a partnership. The same approach also works for members of the community and other significant adults in your students' lives. Encouraging and valuing their contributions strengthen and reinforce their involvement.

As you plan for the school year, develop a strategy to encourage and nurture these vital partnerships. You can start on a small scale by—

- holding regular parent meetings and conferences;
- recruiting classroom volunteers to serve as tutors, guest speakers, and general classroom helpers;
- establishing a school-home connection with homework;
- publishing a parent newsletter; and
- welcoming parents, grandparents, or other involved adults to school.

In this section, you will find other suggestions about how to begin this process, including tips on communicating with parents, sharing your ideas with them, and involving them in the mathematics education of their children. Begin formulating your plan by reviewing these suggestions and reflecting on how they might work for you. Develop goals for parental and community involvement, and jot down notes about how you might accomplish these goals. Talk with your mentor and colleagues about their strategies, and seek out additional resources, such as *Involving Families in School Mathematics: Readings from "Teaching Children Mathematics," "Mathematics Teaching in the Middle School," and "Arithmetic Teacher,"* available from NCTM (Edge 2000). Most of all, develop a positive relationship with the families of your students. Doing so is a rewarding experience and well worth the investment of your time.

51

Calling Home:
Keeping in Contact with Students' Families

Laura Brader-Araje

As a new mathematics teacher, I knew that taking on too much and trying to be perfect at everything would leave me only heartache and stress. For this reason, I decided to be selective in my goal setting for the beginning year. Included in my plan was my hope to develop a system to track communications with the parents and guardians of my students. I knew that the primary method of communication between teachers and students' families at that time was the telephone. Thus, keeping track of incoming and outgoing calls to students' homes would be the basis of any system I would devise.

The System

I decided on an index card system, which may sound simple or even archaic, but what a gem this scheme was for me! I taught five classes, and in my system, each class was coded with a different colored card. For example, period 1 was yellow, period 2 was blue, and so on. Each student was initially allocated a single note card, listing his or her name, parents' or guardians' names, and home and work telephone numbers. I alphabetized the cards in a large index card file.

My Proactive Approach

To initiate positive relationships with all these parents, I took a proactive approach; I decided to go to the parents before they came to me. To do so, I tried to make at least five phone calls a day, leaving messages on machines more often than actually hearing another person on the other end of the line: "Hello, my name is Laura Brader, and I am your daughter's new mathematics teacher. I am calling to introduce myself and to touch base. If you ever need anything, please give me a call at school. I look forward to meeting with you!" I could keep my home number unlisted because I was readily available before, during, and after school hours most of the time.

The Benefits

I maintained my calling routine in between returning calls from parents who had specific concerns throughout the year, because the benefits of the system clearly justified the amount of time involved. The index-card system proved useful over the course of the school year for a variety of reasons, including the following:

- I used the index cards to document the date and time of a call, the person with whom I spoke if someone was available, and the purpose of the call. This record gave me evidence to address problems and to use in team meetings with parents.

- The phone calls helped head off many potential problems because they gave me the chance to mention homework attempts, classroom behavior that was becoming disruptive, concerns about absences, and other issues.

- The system prompted me to call all parents over time, more than once, whether or not I had a specific reason to do so. The calls showed that I cared, and I did, about all my students, not just the infamous ones whoes parents receive phone calls each year from all their child's teachers.

- When problems arose and team meetings were called, the documentation on the index cards allowed me to clarify my approaches toward resolution.

- I created the "luxury," as one team member called it, to transform the dreaded phone call home into an opportunity to tell parents that their children had done well on a project or showed great improvement in a particular area. I found that the parents of students who do not cause problems rarely receive timely, positive feedback about their children; my phone calls provided this praise.

- The initial round of phone calls and messages gave me insight into which students erased messages from teachers before their parents came home and which students did not. I came to understand these students' experiences when teachers had "called home" in the past.

Addressing Administrators' Concerns

In my experience, new teachers often find that their actions—and inaction—are under constant scrutiny.

Administrators may ask, "Have parent phone calls been returned?" "Are guardians being notified of excessive absences?" "Do students know why calls are being made to their homes?" The index cards, kept in a box by the telephone, allow new teachers to answer this barrage of questions they will receive in their first nine months on the job.

Closing Thoughts

Calling home keeps me in contact with the parents or guardians of my students and seems to help head off trouble before it starts. Documenting these interactions provides the backup or proof that teachers need in this age of accountability. Finally, a new teacher's attempts to reach out to parents when school starts and to keep in contact with them throughout the year creates a positive impression of the school and bridges the traditional gap between teacher and community.

Building Relationships: People You Should Get to Know

Lori Shumard

As a first-year teacher, one of your most important tasks is to build relationships that will assist you throughout your career. The following paragraphs remind you of some of the people you should get to know.

Custodians

Custodians are essential to the functioning of the school, and teachers are wise to establish relationships with them. Do not ignore custodians when you see them working during the day; learn and use their names. Find out their birth dates, and make a card or a special dessert to show that you remembered. Have your department or the school administration surprise them with small gifts during the holidays. Custodians usually know every person who works on campus and where they can be found at any time of day. They know where supplies are stored and what is available. They also hold the keys to the entire

campus. You might think that you will never need this access, but someday, you may.

Administrative Assistants

Get to know the administrative assistants in your school, especially the one who is in charge of substitute teachers. One day, you may desperately need this person when you are at your worst. You may be ill, have a sick child, or need to prepare for a workshop. Again, learn the names of the administrative assistants; remember them on their birthdays and during special holidays. Be willing to help out by covering classes if necessary. Every nice act you perform will be repaid many times over.

Fellow Teachers at Your School

When you get your schedule, find teachers who are teaching or have taught the same subjects that you have been assigned. They can help you determine how to pace your instruction, share tests, and tell you what methods work best for different lessons. These colleagues will listen to your problems and offer solutions that have worked for them. Most first-year teachers believe that asking questions and seeking advice are signs of failure or incompetence, but the opposite is true. You will make mistakes; no teacher is perfect the first time in front of a class or the hundredth time! When you stop trying to improve, however, you probably need to find another profession. Good teachers always share new ideas and strategies that work, as well as those that do not work. Establish relationships that are based on sharing and receiving. Be willing to ask and to listen.

Guidance Counselors or Support Personnel

Meet the guidance counselors in your school, and find out which groups of students they represent. Do not wait to seek out a counselor if you feel the need to get advice on handling a problem. Counselors can help solve problems with student behavior and determine appropriate placements. When you have a troublesome student, check with the counselors. They may suggest approaches that have worked with the student in the past, or they may be aware of special needs of the student and can advise you on the best way to handle the situation. Counselors are great resources for taking care of problems before they get out of hand.

Teachers Outside the School

Finally, be sure to make contacts among teachers outside your school. You may go to conferences and other school-related activities and meet many colleagues. When you meet others in the profession, ask about their schools. Exchange e-mail addresses and keep in touch. Sometimes, you may become so wrapped up in problems at your school that you forget that others may already have conquered similar problems. Having contacts outside your school enables you to compare and share with impartial listeners. You can also exchange ideas and collaborate to make instructional changes that are beneficial in the classroom. The contacts you make now will be invaluable in the future.

Acknowledgments: I would like to thank Gladis Kersaint for the help that she gave me in the preparation of this article.

Team Teaching in Mathematics

Amy Weber-Salgo

Team teaching in mathematics can be a wonderful experience for you and for your students. Below are some ideas you may want to consider if you are assigned to a team-teaching situation.

Two Heads Are Better Than One!

Team teaching offers a number of advantages for the instructors, including the following:

- By sharing your teaching ideas, your lessons become more powerful. You and your co-teacher will learn a great deal from each other.

- Although occasionally both teachers will lead a lesson, most of the time, one teacher leads and the other is available for other tasks. Such tasks might include helping students who need extra attention, academically or behaviorally; leading small groups of students who need enrichment or reteaching; performing individual assessments; or simply dealing with other classroom duties.

Communication: The Most Important Aspect of Team Teaching

Each partner must be willing to share both the good news and the problems that arise in the classroom. Here are some issues to discuss before you begin working together in the classroom:

- When do you like to plan—before or after school? On the weekends?

- Do your plans detail all the activities for the entire month, or do you just sketch out each day as it comes? Do your plans fall somewhere in between these extremes?

- Do you want to divide the lessons and have each teacher plan only his or her part, or do you both want to know details about each other's lessons?

- How do you like your classroom to appear? Are you a stickler for neatness, or is a little bit of clutter acceptable?

- How do you plan to buy materials that are not provided by the school? Do you want to have a fund to which you both contribute?

- Do you want to combine all your teaching materials or try to keep them separate?

- How do you like to communicate with parents? How often?

- What is your method for grading?

- How do you like the classroom to sound? Can you tolerate a certain level of noise?

- How do you feel about routines and schedules? Are you comfortable with changes? How will you handle spontaneity and teachable moments?

- How will you resolve conflicts?

You might try rating the importance of issues that arise on a scale of 1–10. If the level of importance is a 9 for your partner and a 3 for you, then give in! If it is a 10 for both of you, then keep working to resolve your differences. Chances are, if the issue is of high importance to both of you, then it is also important to your students. Remember, building this relationship with your co-teacher can be a positive experience. Many of your colleagues would rather share the experience of team teaching than handle their classes alone!

"CLASSY TIPS"

IDEAS FOR ROVING TEACHERS: "CLASSY TIPS" FROM *MATHEMATICS TEACHER* JOURNAL

Kathleen Chadwick (items 1–2)
Ellen Hook (items 3–6)
Jan Shetzler (items 7–21)

Often, beginning teachers are assigned to teach in three, four, or perhaps five different classrooms throughout the school. For example, as a new teacher, one editor of this volume taught on three floors in two different wings of her school building; she found herself in a driver's education classroom; two biology classrooms, complete with critters; a history classroom; and a business classroom. Simply stated, being a rover presents many challenges to a first-year teacher. If you find yourself in this situation, the tips that follow will help you address some of the issues brought on by your "nomadic" status. The ideas come from veteran teachers and are reprinted from the "Classy Tips" column of the September 1998 *Mathematics Teacher* journal.

1. When I was a roaming teacher, I needed an overhead projector on a cart for each floor where I had classes. The cart had a locking door and two shelves inside for my belongings.

2. The important tip is to keep a sense of humor and to try to get your rooms as close together as possible. My alias became "the bag lady," since I always seemed to have one or two with me

3. Keep teacher's editions of the textbooks needed in each classroom where the subject is being taught. Do not carry them from class to class.

4. For planning purposes, keep at home a copy of the textbook for each subject.

5. Carry a large organizer, with a large handle, to store such extra items as paper clips, reinforcements, scissors, stapler, chalk, and so forth. Some teachers do not like others going into "their" desks.

6. Every now and then, do something nice for the teacher with whom you share a room. For example, leave a flower or nice note on the desk. It will make for a great relationship all year long!

7. Ask the teacher whose room you will be using for a copy of the classroom rules and a list of places in the room that are off-limits.

8. Request some space in a file drawer, cabinet, or bookshelf to put such items as a basket for papers that are due, your textbook, and other supplies that you might need.

9. Check the clock to see whether it agrees with your watch—especially if the school does not have bells.

10. Ask your department chair or principal for an extra teacher's edition to keep in the room and one to keep at home so that you can cut down on what you need to "schlepp around."

11. Ask the colleague about a specific arrangement for the desks, so that if you do group activities, you can get the room back in order.

12. Find out if the teacher writes assignments on a section of the chalkboard that you should not erase.

13. Make sure that your students understand that you are guests in another teacher's room and, therefore, that teacher's rules are your rules. I usually asked the students to check for damage to the desktop or excessive garbage before class began so that we would not be blamed for it.

14. Clean up the room before leaving.

15. During open house, make sure that parents understand that you travel. They will be less critical about some of the little things and understand why it is so important for their child to be prepared for class with pencils, paper, and textbook.

16. If you have a classroom set of calculators and they must travel with you all day, find some type of caddy for them. A Rubbermaid tray works well.

17. Ask for a room where you can tutor after school. It's best if it can be the same place all the time, for example, the library, guidance office, or computer lab.

18. Have students keep a copy of your schedule in their notebooks. They can then find you if they have to leave before your class or if they arrive late and miss your class.

19. I have a notebook and assignment book in each room, so that students do not have to find me to get the assignment. They can just go to the room and look it up.

20. Be careful about where you put your gradebook and other items; when you are in a room, it is easy to forget your things—or worse—take someone else's belongings with you.

21. Find out where the teacher keeps supplies that you may use, such as chalk, overhead markers, staples, and so on.

Things I Never Learned in Methods Class: Support Staff and Parents

Margaret R. Meyer

Do not take the school secretaries or custodians for granted. Remember their names, and greet them with smiles. Also, remember to express appreciation for the work they do.

Do not call parents with only bad news. Make sure you get in touch to report students' achievements or hard work. Tell parents how much you enjoy having their child or children in your class.

Sharing Your Principles and Standards with Parents

Mark W. Ellis
Robert Q. Berry III

We have found that most parents, when well informed about a teacher's motives and methods, are supportive of efforts to promote higher-order thinking, conceptual understanding, mathematical communication, and authentic problem solving in the classroom. Many parents see these efforts as a refreshing change from the focus on algorithms they experienced in learning mathematics, which they may remember as a series of unrelated procedures that mysteriously transformed numbers into answers.

To generate parental support, you need to communicate the mathematical goals that you have set for students and the ways in which you are helping students achieve these goals—in essence, your own principles and standards. To help parents become knowledgeable about these goals, you may wish to send home a parent newsletter or make a presentation at a PTA meeting or school open house. You might also create an opportunity for parents to share in the mathematical experiences that their children are receiving in your classroom by hosting a family mathematics night.

These outreach efforts are important because parents who have experienced mathematics through traditional procedure-oriented instruction often have questions about teaching strategies that you may apply in your classroom, for example, cooperative work, student inquiry, manipulative modeling, and writing assignments. Also, consider sharing with parents research findings that support NCTM Standards–based instruction. Parents will see firsthand how Standards-based practices enhance students' understanding and enable them to attach meaning to mathematical concepts and ideas.

Notes:

_____

_____

_____

_____

_____

_____

_____

_____

_____

_____

_____

_____

ONLINE RESOURCES FOR THE BEGINNING TEACHER

The Internet is one of the best resources available to you as a beginning teacher. As you probably already know, numerous Web sites are available for practically any instructional topic in which you are interested. A few sites serve as central clearinghouses, providing links to related sources of information. The Web sites listed below have been active for a while; they are fairly stable in terms of accessibility and are kept up-to-date with the latest educational developments. As part of your professional growth plan, explore these sites to search for information on particular topics or issues pertaining to mathematics teaching and learning. Make an attempt to visit at least one every month, if for no other reason than to learn what is happening in the educational world outside your classroom.

- For professional growth opportunities, visit the National Council of Teachers of Mathematics (NCTM) site at http://www.nctm.org. NCTM membership is required to gain access to some of the features.

- For instructional ideas, visit the Math Forum Web site at http://mathforum.org/. In particular, you might want to explore "Teacher2Teacher" for answers to your questions about teaching mathematics. You can browse the archives, search the frequently asked questions, or submit a question of your own.

- For professional publications related to the implementation of curriculum and instruction, visit the Association for Supervision and Curriculum Development site at http://www.ascd.org.

- For assessment information, view the searchable online journal *Practical Assessment, Research and Evaluation* at http://www.ericae.net/pare.

- For current research publications, browse the education category of the National Academies Press Web site at http://www.nap.edu.

- For a variety of publications related to education, visit the Eisenhower National Clearinghouse site at http://www.enc.org.

- For research and resources on general topics pertaining to various aspects of education, visit the U.S. Department of Education on the Web at http://www.ed.gov.

Notes:

REFERENCES

Baker, Colin. *Foundations of Bilingual Education and Bilingualism.* Philadelphia, Pa.: Multilingual Matters, 2001.

Briggs, Raymond. *Jim and the Beanstalk.* New York: PaperStar, 1970.

Carle, Eric. *The Very Hungry Caterpillar.* New York: Philomel Books, 1969.

Clement, Rod. *Counting on Frank.* Milwaukee, Wis.: Gareth Stevens, 1991.

Crannell, Annalisa. "Collaborative Oral Take-Home Exams." In *Assessment Practices in Undergraduate Mathematics*, edited by B. Gold, S. Z. Keith, and W. A. Marion, pp. 143–45. Washington, D.C.: Mathematical Association of America, 1999.

Edge, Douglas, ed. *Involving Families in School Mathematics: Readings from "Teaching Children Mathematics," "Mathematics Teaching in the Middle School," and "Arithmetic Teacher."* Reston, Va.: National Council of Teachers of Mathematics, 2000.

Feiman-Nemser, Sharon. "What New Teachers Need to Learn." *Educational Leadership* 60 (May 2003): 25–29.

Flores, Alfinio. "Electronic Technology and NCTM Standards." 1998. http://mathforum.org/technology/papers/papers/flores.html (accessed 12 April 2001).

Halliday, Michael Alexander Kirkwood. *Language as Social Semiotic.* Baltimore, Md.: Edward Arnold, 1978.

Kroll, Diana Lambdin, Joanna O. Masingila, and Sue Tinsley Mau. "Grading Cooperative Problem Solving." In *Emphasis on Assessment,* edited by Diana V. Lambdin, Paul E. Kehle, and Ronald V. Preston, pp. 50–57. Reston, Va.: National Council of Teachers of Mathematics, 1996.

National Council of Teachers of Mathematics (NCTM). *Curriculum and Evaluation Standards for School Mathematics.* Reston, Va.: NCTM, 1989.

———. *Principles and Standards for School Mathematics.* Reston, Va.: NCTM, 2000.

Paul, Ann Whitford. Eight Hands Round: *A Patchwork Alphabet.* New York: Harper Collins Publishers, 1991.

———. *The Seasons Sewn: A Year in Patchwork.* New York: Harcourt, 1996.

Renard, Lisa. "Setting New Teachers Up for Failure…or Success." *Educational Leadership* 60 (May 2003): 62–64.

United States Department of Education. *Introduction to TIMSS: The Third International Mathematics and Science Study.* Washington, D.C.: United States Department of Education, 1997.

Notes:

Two additional titles are planned for the
Empowering the Beginning Teacher of Mathematics
series
(Michaele F. Chappell, series editor):

Empowering the Beginning Teacher of Mathematics in Middle School
Edited by Michaele F. Chappell and Tina Pateracki

Empowering the Beginning Teacher of Mathematics in Elementary School
Edited by Michaele F. Chappell, Jane F. Schielack, and Sharon Zagorski

Please consult
www.nctm.org/catalog
for the availability of these titles,
as well as for a plethora of
resources for teachers of mathematics
at all grade levels.

For the most up-to-date listing of NCTM resources on topics of interest to mathematics educators, as well as information on membership benefits, conferences, and workshops, visit the NCTM Web site at www.nctm.org.